THE HERMITAGE

A STROLL AROUND THE HALLS AND GALLERIES

AN ILLUSTRATED GUIDE-BOOK

P-2 Art Publishers

ST PETERSBURG

2008

Foreword by Mikhail Piotrovsky

Introduction by Vladimir Matveyev

Selection and text by Sergei Vesnin, Sophia Kudriavtseva and Tatyana Pashkova

English translation by Paul Williams

Designed by Nikolai Kutovoy

Colour correction by Liubov Kornilova

Computer type-setting by Yelena Morozova

Photographs by Darya Bobrova, Leonid Bogdanov, Pavel Demidov,

Sergei Falin, Alexander Gronsky, Leonard Kheifets, Victor Savik,

Georgy Shablovsky, Vladimir Terebenin and Oleg Trubsky

Edited by Maria Lyzhenkova and Valery Fateyev (English translation)

Managing editor Sergei Vesnin

STROLLING THROUGH THE HERMITAGE

The name of our museum comes from the French and means "a place of solitude". The times when it was the Tsar's private museum are long past, yet even today the Hermitage with its millions of visitors each year is one of the few places where it is possible to find solitude in a dialogue with world culture and Russian history. It is more than just contact with the sublime taking us away from everyday concerns: the Hermitage has its own special atmosphere that awakens the finest elements in the human spirit.

In the Hermitage you can breathe in different cultures, be fascinated by their distinctive features. You can admire masterpieces that stand above all national and cultural differences. You can reflect on episodes in Russian history, many of which took place, at least in part, within these walls.

The Hermitage is to a large extent a unique museum precisely because the history of the world embodied in its cultural attainments is here fascinatingly interwoven with the spirit of our own, Russian history. The ghosts of great artists, famous and anonymous, wander the halls of the Hermitage together with the shades of tsars and courtiers, soldiers and diplomats, writers and revolutionaries, who have left a living memory of themselves here for ever. The museum is so huge and the impressions it generates so varied that it takes many visits to get to know it. Strolling through the Hermitage is probably the greatest pleasure it offers us: to pass unhurriedly from hall to hall, from the historical state rooms to the masterpieces of Ancient sculpture or Dutch painting, thinking as you go about Matisse or Napoleon, Rembrandt or Stolypin, and, inevitably, about Catherine, whose will and taste brought the museum into being. Such a stroll is always full of surprises, even for those who know the Hermitage well. Your eye is suddenly caught by an elaborately carved chair you never noticed before. The sun falling in a different way gives a new vision of a familiar painting. You wander into one of the many temporary exhibitions held in the Hermitage. On the other hand, if works have been removed for exhibition elsewhere, their place might be taken by others from the museum stores. The Hermitage is inexhaustible and generous to those who love it. You can come here with a specific aim, or just to wander wherever the fancy takes you. In the Hermitage you can be constantly gazing from side to side or lost in your own thoughts. You can view the paintings and statues, but equally you can admire the floors and ceilings. You can make your way slowly, taking in every detail, or quickly, eager to reach some favourite, familiar spot. Yet there are few spectacles in the world more attractive than the views from the Hermitage windows: the Neva with the Peter and Paul Fortress and the Spit of Vasilyevsky Island, Palace Square, the Admiralty... The Hermitage entices, fascinates, charms. It never disappoints anyone.

The Hermitage is an extensive museum with many layers to it. It has everything: both spiritual enrichment and new knowledge for any visitor — child, teenager, preoccupied adult, and thoughtful pensioner. The museum is as welcoming to refined intellectuals and inexperienced provincials as it is to venerable scholars, to those still studying and discovering the world and those who are certain they have penetrated its deepest secrets. The Hermitage is equally open to all. Although an aristocrat and a snob, the Hermitage is the most democratic of museums, one where everyone finds something for his or her self.

The Hermitage has lived a very long and complicated existence. It has experienced wars and revolutions, fires, thefts, sales, neglect and lack of understanding. It has also known the emotional uplift of construction and the gambles involved in collecting, the pleasure and pride of saving something, self-sacrificing love and fanatical adoration. Losses and gains, failures and achievements — all of them are to be found in the life of the Hermitage today as well.

For more than 200 years the museum has carried out its sacred duty to be the guardian and curator of world culture on Russian soil. The Hermitage has itself become one of the most characteristic features of the Russian cultural tradition — its universality fused with uniqueness.

It always has something to say to those who visit, no matter how many times they have been. Welcome to the Hermitage.

Mikhail Piotrovsky
Director of the Hermitage

←
*View of the Winter Palace
from Palace Square*

*New Hermitage
The Raphael Loggias*

→
*Winter Palace
The Malachite Room*

The Hermitage is among the greatest museums in the world. Its fame is founded in equal measure on the majestic architectural ensemble, the outstanding collections of objects of art and culture from around the world, and an extremely rich past which is bound up with the foundation, rise and decline of the main imperial residence in St Petersburg. These three facets determine the museum's outstanding significance for Russian and world culture.

The Hermitage owes its origins to the creative and educational activities of the Russian rulers. The winter residence of the Russian monarchs became the centre around which a great museum, its architectural complex and its countless artistic treasures crystallised.

The successive Winter Palaces of Peter the Great, which stood on the site now occupied by the Hermitage buildings, established the pattern of constructing palaces on the main embankment of the new capital. Empress Anna Ioannovna, who reinstated St Petersburg as the capital in 1732, preferred the luxurious mansion of the late Admiral-General Fiodor Apraxin that stood a short distance away, by the Admiralty, but she decided not to break with tradition and move her residence from the bank of the Neva. On her orders a new riverside wing was built onto Apraxin's mansion and this determined the location of the residence for the future. In the years 1754–62, commissioned by Empress Elizabeth, Rastrelli created on the same site the Winter Palace that we see today. Catherine the Great, who took the imperial throne in 1762, immediately set about changing the layout and decoration of the rooms in the Winter Palace. It was her idea to construct the Small and Old Hermitages alongside the official

residence to house her growing art collections. Between 1764 and 1787, on the Empress's orders, the Small Hermitage and then the Large (Old) Hermitage were constructed along the embankment, while the Raphael Loggias block was built onto the latter along the Winter Canal. This was followed in 1783–87 by the construction, a little further up the Neva, of the Hermitage Theatre, linked to the Old Hermitage by an arched aerial walkway. In Catherine II's enlightened age, then, a whole group of buildings appeared by the Winter Palace that became known by the general name of "the Hermitage".

The last element was added to the architectural complex in the middle of the nineteenth century. In 1839 Emperor Nicholas I decided to create one more building for the museum of art on a plot of land adjoining the Winter Canal. After its completion in 1852 this became known as the New Hermitage.

While the Hermitage can trace its architectural history back to the first Winter Palaces of Peter the Great, the history of the Hermitage as a museum collection is traditionally held to have begun in 1764. It was in that year that 225 paintings acquired on Catherine II's orders from the Berlin merchant Gotzkowsky arrived on the banks of the Neva. We do not know the exact date when this collection arrived, but the birthday of the Hermitage is celebrated each year on 7 December, the feast day of St Catherine (in honour of its founder).

Following Gotzkowsky's collection, works of great artistic value were acquired for the Empress across the whole of Europe. This process was furthered by the advice and practical assistance of connoisseurs of art (Dmitry Golitsyn, Alexei Musin-Pushkin, Denis Diderot, Melchior Grimm and many others), as well as the Empress's own undoubted taste. Catherine's Hermitage absorbed the collections of the Prince de Ligne and Count Cobenzl from the Low Countries, Count Brühl from Saxony, Baron Crozat from France, Sir Robert Walpole from England... The museum's stocks grew with extraordinary speed. The first catalogue of the painting collection, published in 1774, already listed some 2,000 works. Apart from paintings, Catherine acquired a host of drawings, engravings, numismatic items, collections of cameos and intaglios, and books, including the libraries of Diderot and Voltaire.

Under Catherine's successors the collections continued to grow. Among the most valuable additions made in the early part of the nineteenth century were the contents of the Malmaison Gallery, formerly the property of Napoleon's first wife, Empress Josephine, acquired by Alexander I; the collection of the Amsterdam banker Coesevelt, and part of that of King William II of the Netherlands, purchased on the orders of Nicholas I.

Nicholas I, who initiated the construction of the New Hermitage, is also connected with the beginning of the tragic practice of mass sales from the Hermitage collections. The Emperor identified a group of paintings that, in his personal opinion, were of little artistic worth and more than a thousand of them were sold at auction. The Hermitage was divested of many of its treasures and subsequently managed to recover only a handful (for example, Chardin's celebrated *Still Life with the Attributes of the Arts*).

Outstanding among the acquisitions of the second half of the nineteenth century and the beginning of the twentieth are two works by Leonardo da Vinci (the *Litta Madonna* was bought in 1865, the *Benois Madonna* in 1914), Basilewsky's collection of mediaeval art, and Semenov-Tian-Shansky's collection of Dutch and Flemish painting.

The First World War and the revolution of 1917 sealed the fate of the main imperial residence. In the summer of 1917 the Winter Palace became the setting for meetings of the Provisional Government. The storming of the palace in October and the overthrow of the Provisional Government opened a new chapter in the history of the former home of the Russian Tsars. A decree of the Military Revolutionary Committee issued on 30 October (Old Style) 1917 declared the Winter Palace to be "a state museum on a par with the Hermitage" and its halls began to be gradually taken over to house the displays of newly-created departments of the Hermitage.

The Hermitage's existence in the post-revolutionary years was full of tragic occurrences. Only towards the end of 1920 did the museum manage to recover its main collections which had been evacuated to Moscow following the outbreak of the First World War and which the Soviet government, having itself moved to Moscow in 1918, considered might be left permanently in the new-old capital. In the event only part of the collection of Old Masters was transferred from the Hermitage to Moscow, for permanent keeping in the Pushkin Museum of Fine Arts. In exchange the Hermitage received from Moscow a share of the works from the collections of Sergei Shchukin and Ivan Morozov. In the 1920s the practice of forming and expanding numerous museums across the USSR by drawing on the stocks of the Hermitage became established and as a consequence many thousands of works went elsewhere. The same period also saw the beginning of the sale of masterpieces from the Hermitage painting collection and works of applied art to buyers abroad. These sales did not, of course, solve the state's financial problems, but they inflicted irreparable damage on the museum. The Hermitage managed to stop the trade in its paintings only in 1934. A reminder of these tragic losses was the opportunity to see Jan van Eyck's *Annunciation*, one of many works sold abroad by the Soviet government, that was kindly returned for a temporary exhibition in 1997 by the National Gallery, Washington.

Severe trials awaited the Hermitage during the Second World War. Before the besieging enemy completely encircled Leningrad, the staff managed to load two trains, sending a considerable part of the museum's collections to the Urals for safekeeping in the Sverdlovsk Picture Gallery. Many items, however, spent all 900 days of the siege in the cellars and ground floor of the museum. Although wounded by bombs and shells, the Hermitage stood firm. In October 1945 the Hermitage collections returned from evacuation and soon the museum reopened its doors to visitors. The restoration of the war-damaged buildings and interiors would take many years, however.

At the same time as the museum was suffering losses in the post-revolutionary years, new directions in research and exhibition activity were being developed within its walls, and new collections being formed. Today the Hermitage is a leading centre of scholarly activity with staff members researching into many aspects of world culture and art. The museum has several research departments, material from whose stocks is included in the permanent display. These are the Departments of the Archaeology of Eastern Europe and Siberia, of the Ancient World, of Western European Art, of the Culture and Art of the Peoples of the East, of the History of Russian Culture, and of Numismatics, as well as the Arsenal, the Menshikov Palace, and the Research Library.

A particular concern for the Hermitage nowadays is to preserve all the wealth of the artistic legacy that it possesses. Specialists of the museum's Department of Scholarly Restoration and Conservation, the staff of the Special Scholarly Restoration Workshops restore thousands of objects of culture and art each year, as well as the priceless Hermitage interiors.

The museum is still constantly expanding its collections. A large share of the acquisitions comes from the Hermitage's archaeological expeditions. Particularly significant collections of archaeological artefacts came into the museum before the late 1980s. The acquisition of new paintings, works of graphic, decorative and applied art, and numismatic items is managed by the Expert Purchasing Commission. A large and particularly important group of new acquisitions comprises the generous gifts of the artists themselves and donations from collectors.

One of the highest priorities in the Hermitage's activities is given to exhibition work. Each year at least twenty temporary exhibitions are held in the museum halls. The tradition of arranging large thematic exhibitions in cities around Russia has been revived.

The Hermitage is actively engaged in the exchange of temporary exhibitions with museums abroad. Thanks to this process, in recent years visitors to the Hermitage have been able to acquaint themselves with outstanding works of world art from collections in Western Europe, the United States and Japan.

Recently the International Club of Friends of the Hermitage has been created. National Friends of the Hermitage societies are active in the Netherlands and the United States. Their aims are to strengthen ties with the museum and to support its efforts to preserve the works of culture and art contained within its walls, as well as the whole architectural complex of the museum.

The Hermitage today is not frozen in its evolution; on the contrary, it is an example of a progressively developing museum. The Menshikov Palace on Vasilyevsky Island, which opened its doors to visitors in 1981, has been accorded the status of a branch of the Hermitage. In recent years the museum has been given the "Spare House" — the next building after the Hermitage Theatre on Palace Embankment (the museum's restoration laboratories are beginning to move into it), and also the building once occupied by the Ministries of Foreign Affairs and Finance, where after a thorough reconstruction it is planned to create a Museum of Decorative Art and a computer education centre for all the city's schoolchildren. The annexation of the General Staff building and the organisation of a new entry point for visitors through the Main Gate of the Winter Palace from Palace Square are steps in the collaboration between the Hermitage, the municipal administration and the command of the St Petersburg military district with the aim of developing the entire Palace Square area as a museum-and-ceremonial complex. On 27 May 1998 (the anniversary of the city's foundation) the colourful ceremony of changing the guard at the Winter Palace was reinstated.

At present work is being completed on the Hermitage's new Restoration and Storage Centre in the Staraya Derevnya district. After it opens, the public will have access to many of the museum's stocks. Excursions will take visitors through the rooms where carriages and furniture, easel and monumental paintings are stored. The creation of such a significant cultural institution in the northern districts of St Petersburg will enable the museum to expand the scale of its activities in the field of public education.

In view of the national and international importance of the Hermitage the museum has been included in the list of especially valuable objects of the cultural inheritance of the peoples of the Russian Federation.

And so, on the threshold of the twenty-first century, while preserving the best traditions of one of Russia's oldest museums and remaining a treasure-house of culture and art, the Hermitage looks confidently into the future.

Vladimir Matveyev,
Deputy Director of the State
Hermitage with responsibility
for exhibitions and development

THE WINTER PALACE

The collections of works of art, gathered together and displayed in the museum known as the Hermitage, are rightly famous around the world. The buildings occupied by the museum today — the Winter Palace, Small, Large and New Hermitages — form one of the most brilliant architectural ensembles in the central part of St Petersburg, an ensemble that was a century and a half in the making. Here in the Hermitage complex history presents itself in all its many aspects; the various facets of the buildings' existence merging together. Visitors find themselves at one and the same time in the exhibition halls of one of the greatest museums on the planet, in a special world of architectural settings designed by some remarkable figures, and in a unique historical monument — the former residence of the Russian monarchs.

*Louis Tocquet. **Portrait of Empress Elizabeth Petrovna**. 1758*

The heart of the Hermitage complex is the Winter Palace, constructed between 1754 and 1762 to the plans of Bartolommeo Francesco Rastrelli (1700–71). The tremendous scale of the building is explained by its intended purpose — to serve as the main residence for the ruler of the Russian Empire. The first Winter Palace appeared in St Petersburg back in the reign of Peter the Great. The choice of the new capital's founder of a site on the bank of the Neva was respected by his successors, successive palaces only shifting closer to the Admiralty. In 1754 Peter's daughter Elizabeth decided on the construction of a new imperial residence. When she died late in 1761, however, the new palace was still not complete and she never lived there. Peter III, who succeeded her, gave orders for the main state rooms and living apartments to be decorated by Easter 1762. The work was carried out and in April the new Tsar and his wife Catherine (the future Catherine II, the Great) moved into the new building. The palace was magnificent. The colours chosen for the façades gave it an exceptional elegance. The walls were painted with "sandy paint with the subtlest shade of yellow, and the ornaments with white lime." The interior decoration was staggering for its richness and variety. The façades of the Winter Palace have generally retained their original appearance (if we disregard the replacement of the sculpture on the parapet in the late nineteenth century and the colour scheme that has changed several times), but the interiors have been repeatedly reworked. Each successive generation of the imperial family adapted the living apartments to its own needs.

Today's Winter Palace preserves the memory of various eras: the creations of Rastrelli's strikingly whimsical architectural fantasy; the state rooms that remind us of official ceremonies; the living apartments decorated in the second half of the nineteenth century drawing on an immense range of architectural prototypes.

The Main Staircase was designed by Rastrelli and when Vasily Stasov restored the interior after the fire of 1837 he adhered to his predecessor's magnificent concept. The theatrical effect here stirs the imagination: the low first flight of the staircase is in shadow and contrasts with the main section where space seems to open out, reflected in mirrors and bursting out into the infinity of the illusory painting on the vault. The painted canvas attached to the ceiling in 1839 is by the eighteenth-century Italian artist Gasparo Diziani and originally adorned one of the halls of Rastrelli's Winter Palace. This composition, depicting Mount Olympus, together with the sculptural allegories of Loyalty, Fairness, Majesty, Wisdom, Justice and Abundance placed in niches pointed to the special function of the palace as the dwelling place of earthly gods, the home of the virtues. The staircase gives access to two suites of state rooms, one along the Neva, the other, main suite, leading to the St George Hall and the Great Church. Walking through this main suite we follow the course taken by cere-monial processions from the mid-nineteenth to early twentieth centuries.

The Peter the Great Hall or Small Throne Room is dedicated to the memory of the founder of the Russian Empire. The hall was created in 1833 to the design of Auguste de Montferrand (1786–1858) and restored practically without changes by Stasov after the fire. The dominant feature of the room is the allegorical painting *Peter the Great and Minerva* by Jacopo Amiconi. Monograms of Peter the Great, crowns and double-headed eagles — symbols of imperial power — are prominent in the decoration of the hall. Paintings depicting the Battles of Poltava and Lesnaya, two key moments in the Northern War, earned the hall the epithet "palladium of Russian greatness and glory" (Clausen). Each successive room in this suite represents one more link in a complex chain of symbolism glorifying Mother Russia.

The Armorial Hall, created by Stasov, was a reminder of the structure of the state. Originally sculpted figures of Russian warriors stood here holding spears

on the shafts of which were the coats-of-arms of the Russian provinces. Gilded shields bearing the same devices can still be seen on the bronze chandeliers.

The Gallery of 1812 — the most famous of the memorial rooms in the palace — was constructed to a design by Carlo Rossi (1775/77–1849) and ceremonially opened on 25 December 1826, the anniversary of Napoleon's army being driven from Russian soil. The 332 portraits installed here are of those who held the rank of general during the war or were promoted to that rank when it ended. Thirteen places were left empty for dead heroes and others whose likenesses could not be found. Alexander I commissioned the portraits from George Dawe. The Russian Emperor met the fashionable English portrait-painter in the German city of Aachen where the first congress of the Holy Alliance (countries involved in the defeat of Napoleon) took place in the autumn of 1818. When he came to St Petersburg, besides his official work for the Gallery of 1812, Dawe was literally deluged with commissions from members of the capital's high society and as a result his stay in Russia lasted from 1819 to 1829. All the portraits were saved from the fire in 1837 and later returned to their places. Dawe's depiction of Alexander I was replaced by a grander equestrian portrait of the Emperor painted by Franz Krüger. The gallery formed a fitting prelude to entering the "heart" of the Winter Palace — the St George Hall.

The St George Hall or the Large Throne Room is where the symphony of magnificent architectural settings reached its climax. The new throne room

The Silver Throne of Empress Anna Ioannovna

The State (Jordan, or Ambassadors') Staircase

The Hall of Peter the Great

The Armorial Hall

was created for Catherine II in 1787–95 by Giacomo Quarenghi (1744–1817) in a special extension built onto the palace within the great courtyard.

The decoration of the throne room in Rastrelli's Winter Palace was never fully completed as Catherine found the opulent whimsy of the Baroque old-fashioned and out of tune with the rational ideals of the Age of Enlightenment. The new throne room was decorated in strict Classical manner. The immense hall with two tiers of windows astonished contemporaries, but Quarenghi's masterpiece perished in the fire of 1837. Emperor Nicholas I gave orders to "try to make the St George Hall … entirely of white marble" and consequently Stasov did not restore the facing of the walls and columns in various different shades of marble. The white Carrara marble that endows the throne room with such an air of solemn grandeur was brought specially from Italy.

George Dawe
Portrait of Nikolai
Rayevsky

George Dawe
Portrait of Alexei
Yermolov.
Before 1824

The ceiling was adorned with gilded ornamentation, the pattern of which is repeated in a parquet floor made of sixteen kinds of colourful wood. Due to the amount of work involved in the marble facing, Stasov completed the St George Hall later than the other restored rooms and it was consecrated in 1841.

The hall played its part in all the official history of Russia's ruling house. The "great entrees" of the imperial family — formal processions from the private apartments through the state rooms of the Neva and Main Suites — ended either in the Large Throne Room or in the Great Church.

The Great Church, elevated to the status of a cathedral in 1807, was created by Rastrelli at the time of the palace's construction and consecrated to the Resurrection in 1762. In 1763, when an icon of the

←
George Dawe. **Portrait of General Piotr
Bagration**. Ca 1823

The Gallery of 1812

George Dawe. **Portrait of Field Marshal Mikhail Kutuzov**. 1829

*The throne
in the St George Hall*

Vernicle (a traditional, supposedly miraculous image of Christ) was installed here, it was reconsecrated as the Church of the Vernicle. After the great fire Stasov was instructed to restore the church to its former appearance. The architect strove to recreate the Baroque elements and follow Rastrelli's original concept. He gave the church back its dome that had been covered over long before the fire. A large part of the decoration here was produced in papier-mâché that provided a useful alternative to time-consuming wood-carving in view of the brief period allotted to the restoration of the Winter Palace. The idea of using this material first occurred to Stasov in 1820 when he was restoring the palace church at Tsarskoye Selo. The splendid iconostasis by the master carver Cretan was disassembled in the 1940s.

A small passageway connects the state rooms to the living area of the Winter Palace. These, once the private dwelling place of all the Russian rulers and their families, from Catherine II to Nicholas II, the quarters for ladies- and gentlemen-in-waiting, and ancillary rooms, spread over three storeys of the palace now house some of the exhibits that make the Hermitage such a rich museum. The Departments of the Archaeology of Eastern Europe and Siberia, Russian Culture and the East were formed in the Soviet period. Thanks to them, the Hermitage, which had been famous for its outstanding collection of Western European painting since the

The St George Hall

*The bell-tower
of the Great Church*

*The dome
of the Great Church*

*The interior
of the Great Church*

beginning of the nineteenth century, earned the right to be regarded as one of the major repositories of the world's cultural artefacts. The treasures of Scythian burialmounds and Sassanid silver from Iran, Persian carpets and Chinese porcelain, the sculpture of Ancient Egypt and Byzantine icons, coins, jewellery, weapons, ivory, metal and wooden articles, stones worked by Russian craftsmen and the works of celebrated artists of Peter the Great's time. The most precious part of the Hermitage's stocks, first and foremost the Western European painting, came into the museum through the collecting activities of the Russian rulers.

In 1764 Catherine the Great acquired a large collection of paintings by Western European artists from the Prussian merchant Johann Ernst Gotzkowsky and so laid

Etienne Maurice Falconet
Cupid Wagging His Finger. *1757*

Falconet (1716–1791) was a celebrated French sculptor of the Rococo era. In 1767 he came to Russia at the invitation of Catherine II to work on the "Bronze Horseman" monument to Peter the Great. All the works by Falconet now in the Hermitage were created before he left France. This *Cupid* was one of the most popular statues of the eighteenth century, known from a large number of replicas'. The elegant figure of the little god of love, full of easy grace, was commissioned by the sculptor's patroness, the Marquise de Pompadour to decorate a "temple of love" in the garden.

the foundation for the Hermitage's picture gallery. Within a short time the Russian Empress's collection could justly lay claim to one of the first places in the world for both the quantity and the quality of the works that it included.

The "Northern Minerva", as Catherine was known in Europe, sought as quickly as possible to make her holdings the equal of the celebrated royal collections of Vienna and Paris, thus elevating the prestige of the Russian court and her own reputation as an enlightened monarch. As Catherine herself admitted, she understood nothing about painting and relied entirely for the selection of works on intermediaries who included some of the century's most brilliant minds — the philosopher Denis Diderot, the man of letters Melchior Grimm, and the diplomat Dmitry Golitsyn.

During Catherine's reign the Hermitage came into possession of many outstanding paintings, notably first-rate products of the Dutch and Flemish schools, with the oeuvres of Rembrandt, Rubens and Van Dyck particularly well represented. Through the efforts of Diderot superb examples of French seventeenth- and eighteenth-century painting found their way to St Petersburg. Towards the end of the century works by Italian Renaissance artists were acquired, while the Netherlandish, German, Spanish and English schools were represented by outstanding individual pieces.

In the Empress's day all these treasures hung in the halls of the Winter Palace, and also in the buildings of the Small and Large (Old) Hermitages that Catherine had built specifically for them. There, apart from the owner herself, they could be seen only by members of the court, and foreign travellers, artists and students of the Academy of Arts who were granted special permission. By the middle of the nineteenth century the collection of Western European painting had for the most part been formed, but right up to the early twentieth century additions were being made. Today's Hermitage picture gallery bears little resemblance to Catherine the Great's "place of solitude".

The former living quarters and service rooms of the Winter Palace are now given over to collections that cover a period from prehistoric times to the present century: from artefacts uncovered by archaeological excavations and the works of Oriental craftsmen to masterpieces of Western European painting and sculpture.

The strikingly rich and varied collection of French art from the fifteenth to twentieth centuries occupies about fifty rooms in the Winter Palace.

The collection is rightly considered one of the most significant and complete in the Hermitage's stocks. It occupies some fifty rooms in the museum and covers practically all styles and trends in French art, presenting leading painters, sculptors and masters of applied art. No other collection outside of France can compete with the Hermitage for quantity and quality of splendid products of the refined Gallic culture. Many of them were acquired at the instigation of Catherine II who was reckoned a great admirer of French style and French fashion.

The great seventeenth-century artist Nicolas Poussin (1594–1665) — creator and head of the French Classical school — is represented in the Hermitage by twelve works. The greater part of Poussin's life was spent in Italy, far from Paris and the royal court with its strict rules and demands on an artist. In the atmosphere of falsehood and hypocrisy that prevailed at the court of Louis XIII, where the straightforward, noble-minded artist became the target of lies, envy and hatred from his fellows, particularly Simon Vouet, Poussin would never have attained greatness. Only in Italy, a country he adored, could the painter develop freely, following his own aesthetic tastes and convictions. The study of Classical monuments and Renaissance masterpieces coupled with reflection on the character of perfection and harmony in nature and in art led Poussin to create the theory and practice of Classicism — a balanced, elevated style that celebrated the triumph of human reason.

Landscape with Polyphemus (1649) is a glorious dream of an ancient "Golden Age", of a world in which people, gods and animals live in harmony with the natural setting that is beautiful and eternal. It was probably this very work to which Poussin was referring to when he wrote in a letter: "Paintings that possess perfection should not be viewed in haste, but slowly examined, evaluating, and with understanding…"

At first glance the *Dairymaid's Family* by Louis Le Nain (1593–1648) seems a humble scene of daily life in comparison with Poussin's magnificent creations. The painting, produced in the 1640s, belongs to what is known as the peasant genre, of which Louis Le Nain was reckoned the greatest exponent. Yet Le Nain's peasants are full of the same sense of majesty as Poussin's mythological or biblical characters. The figures of the elderly countrywoman, the old man, boy and girl gathered around the donkey that is the mainstay of their existence are superficially almost totally inactive; they are frozen against the background of an immense silvery-blue sky and a distant hilly landscape. Every detail here seems real and accurate in the extreme, but at the same time this relatively small work is full of the true artistry and genuine monumental quality characteristic of the finest examples of French Classicism.

The Hall of French Rococo Art

In the south wing of the palace in 1838–39 Alexander Briullov created a suite of five state rooms in which a collection of battle paintings inspired by events in Russian eighteenth- and nineteenth-century martial history. Originally this area was living quarters, including, alongside the Great Church, the apartments of Catherine the Great. In the south-east, in the attics some exquisitely decorated rooms were created that from the 1780s were used to display oriental curios and objects of applied art. It was these "Chinese" attics that Catherine II called her "hermitage".

Simon Vouet
**Portrait of Anne
of Austria.** *Ca 1643*

Vouet (1590–1649) was
the first painter to King
Louis XIII, one of the
creators of the official,
elevated style. His majestic
canvases on historical and
allegorical subjects are
full of grand, rather cool
rhetoric and bombast.
This portrait is a grand
allegorical depiction of the
Queen, wife of Louis XIII
and mother of the future
Sun-King Louis XIV, in
the guise of Minerva,
the Ancient Roman
goddess of wisdom, with
attributes of power and
wisdom — the helmet,
shield, sceptre and owl.

*Dish. 16th century. France
Workshop of Bernard
Palissy*

Palissy (*ca* 1510–89)
was one of the most
outstanding figures in
France for the breadth
and depth of his
knowledge, a typical
"Renaissance man".
He studied chemistry
and natural sciences, was
a writer, an artist and
a garden architect.
He invented the clear lead
glaze that he used to
create his celebrated
"Palissy ware" — pottery
decorated with reliefs
depictions of frogs, fish,
lizards and snakes.

The suite of rooms running alongside the courtyard of the Winter Palace,
parallel to the displays of French sixteenth- and seventeenth-century art, contains
German art of the fifteenth to eighteenth centuries. This collection cannot lay
claim to the fullness or variety of the French. The age of the German Renaissance is represented here through one of its greatest artists — Lucas Cranach
the Elder (1472–1553). The Hermitage possesses four paintings by Cranach.
Particularly noteworthy among them is *Venus and Cupid* (1509), the artist's
earliest work on the subject. It is believed that this painting was the first attempt
made in northern Europe to depict the goddess of love and beauty naked. In
Germany at the time of the Reformation the image of Venus was associated with
the sin of lechery, hence the Latin inscription towards the top of the work that
warns: "Reject Cupid's sensuality with all your might, else Venus will take
possession of your blinded soul."

On the whole, however, the modest stock of German painting serves to stress even more clearly the wealth and range of the French collection, particularly the eighteenth century. It was at that time that France firmly captured the European art market and the Rococo style that emerged then became the yardstick of taste, elegance and luxury. Celebrated porcelain services produced by the craftsmen of the Sèvres factory, an immense stock of tapestries, exquisite Rococo furniture, and decorative pieces made of bronze and silver give a special atmosphere to the halls that house the works of the greatest artists of the century, the age when French culture triumphed.

The Hermitage can boast eight paintings by Antoine Watteau, twelve by François Boucher, and several first-rate canvases by Jean-Baptiste Siméon Chardin and Jean-Honoré Fragonard. The sculpture of this period is represented by works from its finest masters — Etienne Maurice Falconet and Jean Antoine Houdon.

Antoine Watteau (1684–1721) was the founding father of a style that determined the character of French art in the eighteenth century — the virtuoso artistry of the Rococo. Yet Watteau's paintings, for all their immediately dazzling mastery, are complex and contradictory like the personality of the artist himself. *A Capricious Woman* (*ca* 1718) is considered one of the finest examples what is known as the *fête galante*, a genre invented by Watteau in which the subject revolves around the characters' barely detectable feelings. The painter often left his paintings untitled, stressing the fact that for him the important thing was not a narrative plot, but a particular emotional state expressed by purely painterly means — through rhythm, colour scheme and movement.

The Adoration of the Magi
Central part of a triptych
Early 16th century
Limoges, France. Enamel

Painted enamels, produced primarily for religious purposes — images of saints, folding domestic altarpieces became a speciality of Limoges before the end of the Middle Ages. The technique involved was highly complicated: copper plaques were covered with layer of opaque white enamel. After firing a design was outlined on it with black paint and then painted in with transparent enamel colours. The main difficulty of this process lay in the fact that the piece had to be fired 10–15 times, as each colour required a particular temperature. In the fifteenth century multicoloured enamels were with gold paint and cabochons — large drops of translucent enamel placed on pieces of gold or silver foil in imitation of precious stones.

Louis Le Nain
Dairymaid's Family. 1640s

→
Nicolas Poussin
Landscape with Polyphemus. 1649

The Alexander Hall

In 1834 Alexander Briullov drew up a plan
for a hall dedicated to the memory of
Alexander I that was realised after the
great fire. The architect found a brilliant
spatial and constructional solution for the
immense hall with two tiers of windows.
The original ceiling design with fan vaults
supporting shallow domes became
the chief feature of the Alexander Hall.
The tremendous airiness and the grandeur
of the spaces beneath the domes caused
contemporaries to speak of the room
being " in the Byzantine taste". The hall
perpetuated the memory of Alexander I
(a portrait of the Emperor by George Dawe
was placed on the end wall and above it
a bas-relief depicting Alexander in profile
"in the guise of the Slavonic deity Rodo-
mysl" — the embodiment of wisdom and
courage) and of the "Patriotic War" of 1812
and subsequent foreign campaign by the
Russian army. The frieze was adorned by
enlarged copies of the medals designed
by Fiodor Tolstoi, that tell of those events
in an allegorical way, and symbolic figures
of Glory. The main element in the moulded
decoration are compositions of military
accoutrements. In contrast to the Gallery
of 1812 which recalled specific heroes of
the war against Napoleon, the Alexander
Hall reminded people of that highly important event in Russia history through
images and allusions. The memorial
character of the hall was underlined by
four immense battle scenes painted
by Gottfried Willewalde.

PELLE · CVPIDINEOS · TOTO   CONAMINE · LVXVS
NE · TVA · POSSIDEAT   PECTORA · CECA · VENVS

Lucas Cranach the Elder
Venus and Cupid. 1509

Lucas Cranach the Elder
Female Portrait. 1526

Wedding goblet
15th century
Germany. Silver

Striking mastery, freedom and immediacy in the treatment of his subject were demonstrated by Jean-Honoré Fragonard (1732–1806) in *The Stolen Kiss* (late 1780s). This masterpiece by the darling of the Parisian public — "Frago" as he was affectionately known to his numerous advisors — came into the Hermitage in the late nineteenth century from the former collection of the last King of Poland, Stanislas Poniatowski.

Saying Grace by Jean-Baptiste Siméon Chardin (1699–1779) simply oozes persuasive verisimilitude and naturalness. Yet even in the real world where Chardin's humble heroines have their existence, a French artist of the second half of the eighteenth century managed to find the spirituality, harmony and poetry so characteristic of the works of his great predecessors — Poussin, Le Nain and Watteau.

Adjoining the halls of eighteenth-century French art is a relatively small collection of English art. The paintings and pieces of applied art displayed here nonetheless give an adequate impression of the distinctive qualities of the English school.

English art reached its highest point in the work of two outstanding eighteenth-century painters: Thomas Gainsborough (1727–1788) and Joshua Reynolds (1723–1792). The first president of the Royal Academy and head of the English school, Sir Joshua was celebrated first and foremost for his paintings. Four works in the Hermitage collection give us an idea of the "historical compositions" to

Cameo Service. 1778–79 Sèvres porcelain factory, France

This service, striking for its elegant forms and refined combinations of colour, was produced at the Sèvres factory for Catherine II.

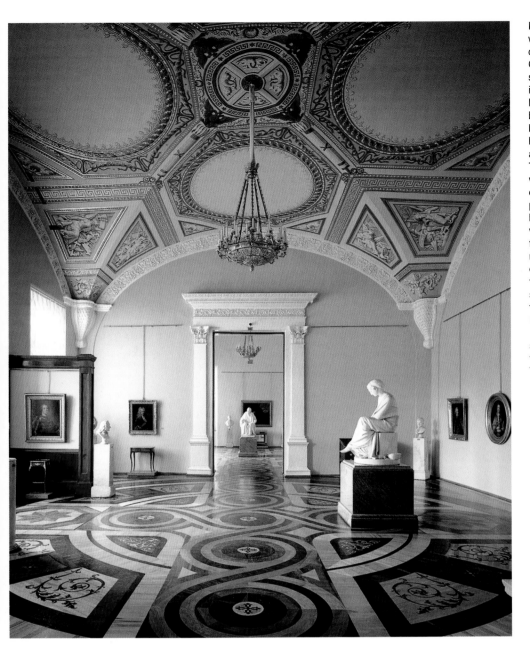

In March 1778 the Empress wrote to her constant correspondent Melchior Grimm: "The Sèvres service that I have ordered is intended for the greatest lover of nail-biting, my dear, beloved Prince Potemkin, but in order that the service be as good as possible I am saying that it is for me." The pieces are decorated with depictions of ancient cameos alternating with plant ornament on a background of turquoise with gilding. Garlands of flowers form the Empress's monogram. During the fire of 1837 about 160 items from this service were stolen. Ten years later they turned up at auction in London. The efforts of Russian diplomats succeeded in returning them to the Winter Palace. Today there are 688 pieces in the Hermitage collection.

The Hall of Eighteenth-Century French Art

Etienne Maurice Falconet
Winter. *1771. Marble*

which the artist turned his hand quite rarely. *Cupid Untying the Girdle of Venus* is one of the artist's own replicas on a popular subject of the day, but the figures in the painting are far removed from the Classical ideal. Venus is an entirely real, flesh-and-blood English beauty, with a rosy complexion and red hair looking out coquettishly at the viewer in feigned bewilderment at the dangerous game being played by the naughty urchin Cupid.

Gainsborough's *Portrait of a Lady in Blue* is marked by the poetic spiritual quality that was the hallmark of this subtle, refined artist. The depiction of the woman on the canvas resembles some exquisite flower created in a harmony of silver, grey and blue tones.

The remarkable collection of French nineteenth- and early-twentieth-century painting housed in third-floor rooms reflects all the complex, at times dramatic struggle between different tendencies, the changes of styles and leaders that

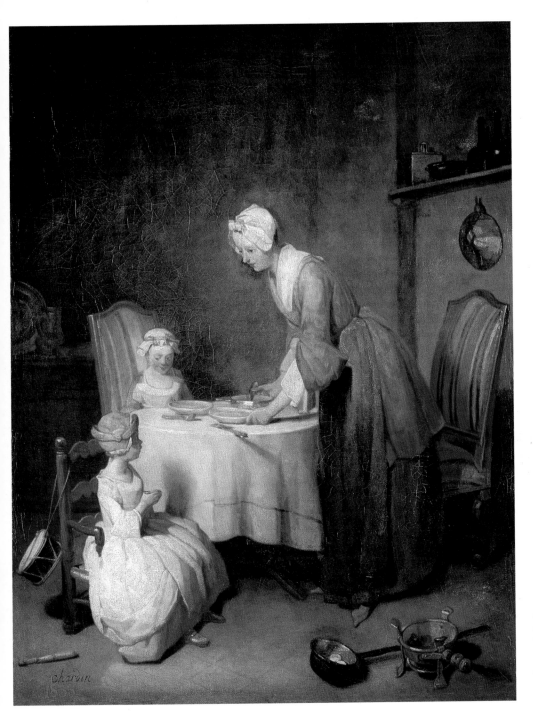

characterized the art of this period. The first tendency, which established itself towards the end of the eighteenth century, on the eve of the French Revolution was Neo-Classicism, represented here by the works of pupils and followers of the school's head, Jacques-Louis David (1748–1825). We can judge the first, revolutionary, stage of the new Classicism from the painting *Napoleon on the Bridge at Arcola* created by one of David's most loyal pupils, Jean Antoine Gros (1771–1835). Artists of this tendency usually painted subjects from the Ancient World, Roman history being especially popular, and sought out examples of fidelity to great ideas. For them Napoleon was practically the only contemporary whose martial deeds in the name of his country could stand alongside those of ancient heroes.

The work by David himself to be found in the Hermitage, *Sappho and Phaon*, belongs to the late stage of Classicism, when the "ancient cries of the revolution" had died down. David became first painter to

Jean-Honoré Fragonard
The Stolen Kiss
Late 1780s

Joshua Reynolds
**Cupid Untying the Girdle
of Venus.** 1788

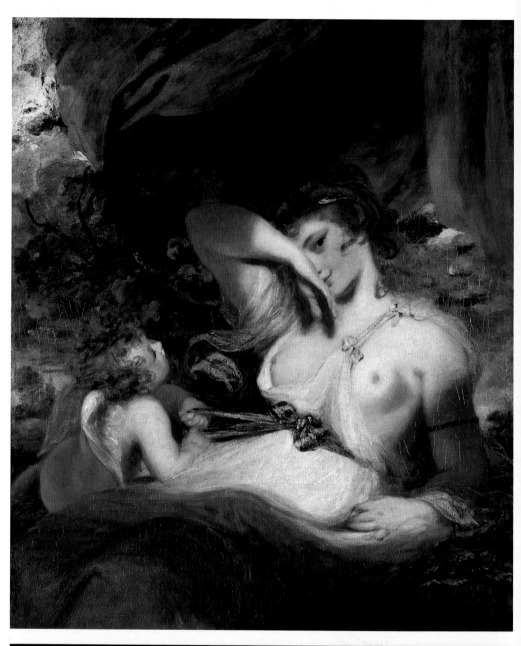

The Green Frog Service
1773–74. Wedgwood
factory, England

Catherine II commissioned
this service for a "wayside
palace" (later called the
Chesme Palace) located
outside St Petersburg on
the road to Moscow.
The locality was known in
the Finnish of the local
peasantry as Kekerekek-
sinen — "the frog marsh".
Hence the emblem on the
service: a green frog on a
heraldic shield. The service
was intended for 50 diners
and included dinner (680
pieces decorated with
garlands of oak-leaves)
and desert (264 pieces
decorated with ivy leaves)
sections. Each item was
individually painted with a
different, true-to-life view of
a place in England. While
working on the service
Josiah Wedgwood (1730–
1795) perfected the traditional English creamware
pottery, calling his variety
"Queen's Ware" in honour
of his patroness Queen
Charlotte.

Thomas Gainsborough
Portrait of a Lady in Blue
Late 1770s

Jacques-Louis David
Sappho and Phaon. 1809

Napoleon, the new Emperor of France. Everything in the painting would seem to follow the traditions of Neo-Classicism — from the ideally beautiful images of the Ancient Greek poetess and her lover to the details of furniture and clothing that David sketched from authentic works of ancient art. But the Ancient World serves here to express tender feelings, rather than extol civic virtues.

The Classical system had a great many adherents in France, but even the most convinced sometimes found themselves constricted by its rigid framework. In the 1820s it collapsed, giving way, not without a fight, to Romanticism. The greatest of the French Romanticists, Eugène Delacroix (1798–1863),

Eugène Delacroix
Lion Hunt in Morocco
1854

Camille Pissarro
**The Boulevard
Montmartre in Paris.** *1897*

Auguste Renoir
**Portrait of the Actress
Jeanne Samary.** *1878*

Claude Monet
The Pond at Montgerond
1876–77

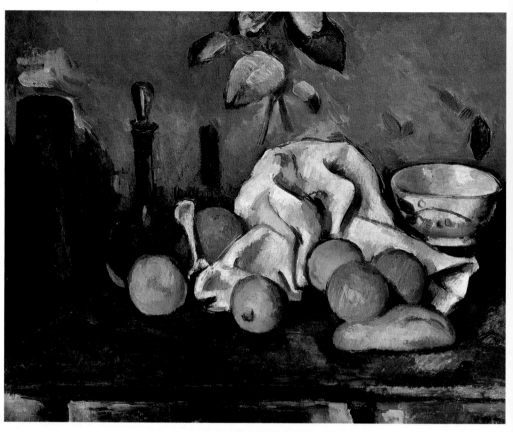

Paul Cézanne
Still Life. Ca 1879–82

Paul Cézanne
Large Pine near Aix
Late 1890s

*Vincent van Gogh. **Cottages**. 1890*

is represented in the Hermitage by two works dating from the 1850s, when Romanticism had long since established its right to exist, yet they still carry the dynamism and energy of that heroic age.

Realism, which succeeded Romanticism, began with the landscapes of the Barbizon school. It was the members of that school, Théodore Rousseau, Jules Dupré, Charles Daubigny, the celebrated master of the landscape Camille Corot, and also the great Realists of the middle of the century, François Millet, Gustave Courbet and Honoré Daumier, who became the true teachers of a new generation of French painters knoun as the Impressionists. The Hermitage's stock of works representing the main trends of the second half of the nineteenth and early twentieth centuries — Impressionism, Post-Impressionism, Fauvism, Cubism — is justly considered one of the finest in the world. Claude Monet and his kindred spirits, Auguste Renoir, Edgar Degas, Camille Pissarro and Alfred Sisley, struggled against the hide-bound traditions of Classical art, striving to regenerate painting by getting closer to nature — a lighter palette, directly conveying impressions from everyday life, yet they did not spurn the great legacy of the artists of the past. The works of Le Nain, Poussin, Watteau, Chardin and Fragonard remained for them great examples for study, the true school by which to master painting. The participants of the first Impressionist exhibition in 1874 also included Paul Cézanne (1839–1906), but in contrast to his fellows there, he did not strive only to convey impressions of the real world. He dreamed of turning Impressionism into a kind of art that would be "eternal, solid, like the art of the museums".

Vincent van Gogh
Lilac Bush. *1889*

Paul Gauguin
Woman Holding a Fruit
1893

Auguste Rodin. **Head of a Man with a Broken Nose.** *Bronze*

The work of Auguste Rodin (1840–1917) opened a new page in the evolution of Western European sculpture in the late nineteenth and early twentieth centuries. The outstanding French sculptor is represented in the Hermitage by pieces from various stages in his career. The collection opens with a plaster cast that was used for the casting in metal of the celebrated statue *The Age of Brass* (*L'Age d'Airain*) that marked the start of Rodin's complex, contradictory path towards the regeneration of plastic form. A number of later works are connected with the concept to which the sculptor devoted his life but which was destined never to be fully realised — the *Gates of Hell*, a cycle of sculptures and reliefs intended to decorate the entrance to the Museum of Decorative Arts in Paris. The sketches became works of art in their own right. Rodin's marble group *Eternal Spring*, known from numerous copies, is probably the most popular example of such a transformation.

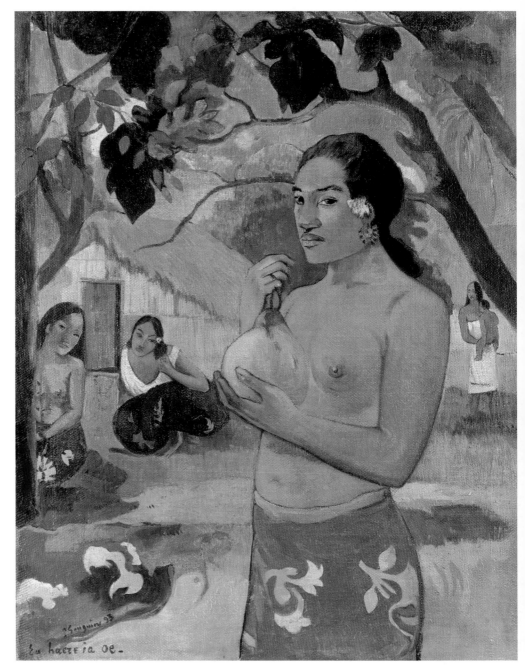

Like the Impressionists, Cézanne worked outdoors, but the objects in his still lifes are not dissolved by the air, turning into patches of colour, but have the same density and material quality as in the works of the Old Masters; only he does not achieve it by gradations of light and shade, but by the alternation of warm and cold colours.

The painting of the tormented Dutch-born Vincent van Gogh (1853–1890) was also to a large extent founded on the achievements, but colour in his paintings is more active than it is in life. For him the colour scheme was above all an expression of the feelings and emotions that possessed him while he worked. In essence Van Gogh used impressions from life as a means to express his own spiritual states. The four Hermitage paintings by Van Gogh were painted in the last, most

NAVE NAVE MOE

Auguste Rodin. **Eternal Spring.** *1897. Marble*

Paul Gauguin
**Sacred Spring
(Sweet Dreams).** *1894*

Paul Signac
The Harbour at Marseilles
1906

In conjunction with Georges Seurat, Paul Signac (1863–1935) developed in the late 1880s a new manner of working that became known variously as Neo-Impressionism, Divisionism or Pointillism. This new Impressionism took the form of painting with small separate (hence Divisionism) dabs of colour and was founded on precise scientific knowledge of physical principles relating to the blending of shades of colour. The Neo-Impressionists contrasted their method to the spontaneity of the Impressionist glimpse of the world.

Henri Rousseau
**The Chopin Monument
in the Jardin du
Luxembourg.** *1909*

Henri Rousseau (1844–
1910), who worked in
the Paris customs office
(hence his nickname
"Douanier Rousseau"),
was a "Sunday painter",
an amateur. But his naive,
sincere art caught the
attention of professional
artists, above all Renoir,
Degas, Gauguin and
Picasso, and eventually
went down in the history
of French art as a sepa-
rate, original phenomenon.
The world of Rousseau's
images is divorced from
reality, although often
inspired by specific events
or places.

*Vase in the form of
a peach-tree trunk with
fruit. 18th century
China. Chalcedony*

Located in the second-floor
rooms of the Winter
Palace, alongside the
collection of later French
art, is a display of Chinese
art spanning a period from
the fourteenth century B.C.
to the twentieth century.
The core of the collection
is superb examples of
Chinese applied art —
porcelain and articles
made from semiprecious
stone and enamel.

*The display of
Impressionist painting*

dramatic period of the artist's life. At Arles in 1888 he painted *Memories of the
Garden at Etten* (1888) and *The Arena in Arles* (1888). In the following year he
produced *The Lilac Bush* in the garden of the hospital at Saint-Rémy. *Cottages*,
created in Auvers-sur-Oise, dates from 1890, the year of his tragic death. Van
Gogh was invited there by Dr. Gachet who took care of the artist in his clinic.

The bright colour scheme of the canvas based on diverse correlations of warm ochreous and cold green-blue shades is full of harmony. Only the sharp and nervous brushstrokes of the deeply mixed colours are dashing from the lower left corner of the painting upwards to merge with the flood of strokes in the upper section of the canvas creating a sense of great inner tension.

The third figure who stands alongside Cézanne and Van Gogh at the sources of twentieth-century art is Paul Gauguin (1848–1903). The three, for all their apparent complete disparity of tastes, passions, origins and education, nonetheless had much in common: as lone rebels they each started from Impressionism and devised their own method. As a result they are customarily known as the Post-Impressionists.

Paul Gauguin began his career as an artist at the age of thirty-five. Even his early independent paintings are filled with symbolism and his new method of representation based on the daring combinations of colour spots skirted by

Pablo Picasso
Woman with a Fan. *1908*

Pablo Picasso
Boy with a Dog. *1905*

*Figurine of a lion
18th century. China
Porcelain, painted in
enamel colours*

lines was reminiscent of the technique of cloisonné enamels (from the French *cloison* – a partition).

Gauguin created his best works on Tahiti – the island of his dream where he wanted to spend his whole life and where he acquired a veritable earthly paradise inhabited by beautiful, natural and free people. He died alone on the small Dominique Island in the Pacific leaving after himself dozens of then unknown masterpieces, which are nowadays the pride of the world's best museums. The Hermitage boasts a large collection of Gauguin's paintings — fifteen canvases created mainly on Tahiti. In the best works of this period the artist achieved at last the harmony he was seeking for in Paris. He regarded the quiet and natural flow of life of the Maori tribe as a Golden Age, in which people live in accord with the natural environment. The landscape in *Tahitian Pastorals* sounds as a powerful chord of bright chromatic spots, while the whimsical, meandering rhythm of lines seems to echo the sounds of the pipe played by the woman seated behind a tree. The colour and linear design are nearly perceptible embodiments of music permeating this real and at the same time fairy-tale, magic realm of Tahitian dreams and visions. The main character of *Woman Holding a Fruit* expresses Gauguin's ideal of beauty. The woman's face is calm and its features are immobile; she resembles a gold-coloured statue carved in wood. At the same time this woman on Gauguin's canvas appears as a majestic and happy being living amidst generous, primordial nature. The subject-matter of Gauguin's Tahitian canvases is sometimes complex and has more than one meaning yet they invariably reveal the great talent of the master, who succeeded in breathing a vivid, highly individual feeling into the most rational and abstract idea.

Pablo Picasso (1881–1973) and Henri Matisse (1869–1954) — two of the greatest artists of the twentieth century —are represented in the Hermitage by some of the finest examples of their work. It was their art that particularly attracted

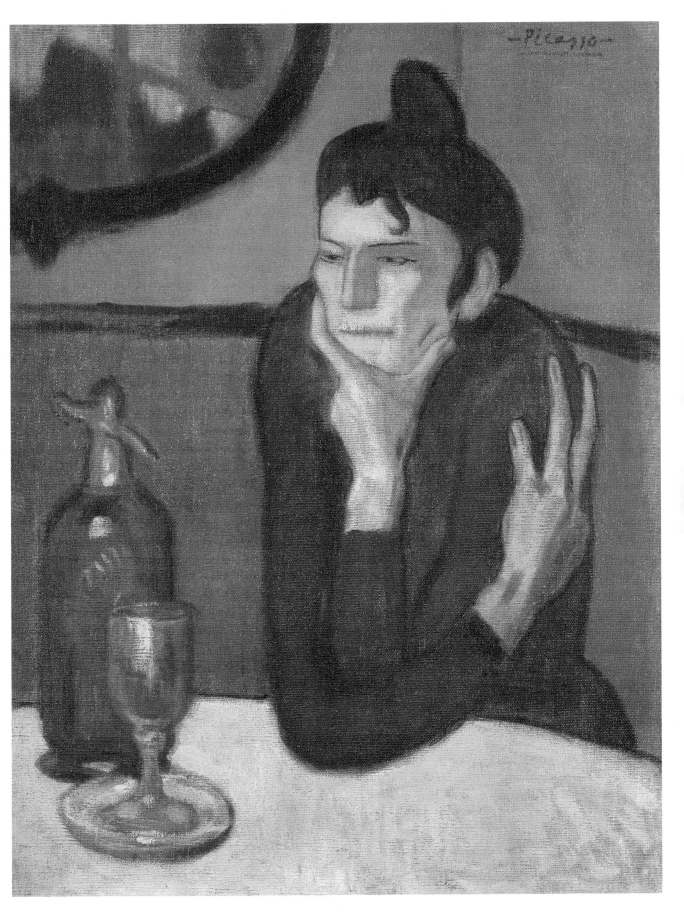

Pablo Picasso. *The Absinth Drinker.* 1901

Henri Matisse. ***The Painter's Family.*** *1911*

the Russian industrialist Sergei Shchukin, who before the First World War bought what seemed their boldest works, puzzling his fellow collectors. It is to Shchukin's collection that we owe all the thirty-plus Picassos in the Hermitage. They date from the three early period of his career — Blue, Pink and Cubist.

The Absinthe Drinker (1901) was painted by the twenty-year-old Picasso soon after he moved from Spain to Paris. The motif, very popular with French artists, here acquires a dramatic, acutely psychological tone uncharacteristic of contemporary French painting. These qualities became even stronger in the works of the Blue Period, so called because of Picasso's predilection for the colour dark blue that expresses feelings of loneliness, melancholy, sadness and suffering shared.

A tragic sense of hopelessness emanates powerfully from *The Visit* (*Sisters*) (1902), one of the key works of the Blue Period.

The story of this canvas gives us an idea of how a real-life impression might inspire Picasso to a composition that can stand comparison with the art of the Old Masters, particularly the Spaniards Ribera, Zurbarán and Morales. Originally Picasso intended to paint the meeting between two sisters, a nun and a prostitute, by the walls of the Saint-Lazare prison hospital. Gradually, however, as he worked on the idea, the indications of time and place grew increasingly abstract. Finally Picasso left on the canvas only two, almost identical female figures dressed in dark blue, rendered ageless, located in a timeless, cold, blue-green space. The tragedy of human loneliness, expressed with extreme drama here, was to be one of the chief themes in Picasso's output.

In 1906 Picasso moved on to Cubism. Now he was creating his own world based on the laws of geometry and logic. On the one hand Cubism is founded of Cézanne's celebrated formula: "everything in nature can be pictured in the form of a sphere, a cylinder and a cone." On the other on the geometrical simplicity and inner freedom of Black African sculpture.

In *Woman with a Fan* (1908) all the details of the face and body are reduced to simplified forms, combinations of curved and straight-edged volumes. Yet this geometrical image, seemingly hewn from hard rock does not lose its emotional impact — the pose, gesture and inclined head express a sense of tiredness and concentration.

Henri Matisse founded his work on the leading role of colour; asserting with each picture the idea that "an artist should possess the gift of colour, like a singer his voice." Like Picasso, he became the creator of a new tendency — Fauvism (from *fauves*, meaning "wild beasts"). In 1905 a group of young artists headed by Matisse caused the official critics to literally explode with disapproval at the Salon d'Automne when they came across their bright, unfettered paintings screaming with tense combinations of paints. Covering his canvas with blue, red and green, bringing them together in jarring chords, Matisse sort after the ultimate concentration of feelings that could be expressed through a patch of colour.

The Red Room (1908) might be called Matisse's programmatic work, one in which all his principles are most precisely expressed. The red colour here is like a musical instrument in an orchestra playing solo. The original composition looked different, though, and was called *Harmony in Blue* with a dominant role being taken by the pale blue drapery.

The artist has turned all the elements of the picture — the still life on the table, the figure of the woman, the table and chairs, and the landscape outside the window — into flat patches of colour, rhythmically echoing the ornament of the decorative fabric that organizes space on the canvas.

Carpet (detail)
5th century B.C.
Pazyryk burial mound

The halls on the ground floor of the Winter Palace contain extremely precious exhibits belonging to the Department of Primitive Culture. First and foremost they are artefacts from burials made by nomadic tribes in the Altai, Siberia and the south of Russia in the fifth and fourth centuries B.C. In the Pazyryk Valley in the Altai between 1927 and 1949 some priceless items were discovered that had been created more than 2,500 years ago and splendidly preserved by the unusual conditions prevailing in the burial mounds. Frozen soil formed beneath the artificial mound of stones. Water permeated into it, but the sun never reached it, creating conditions similar to permafrost. Because of this, the graves of tribal chieftains were found to contain not only stone artefacts, but wooden items, the mummies of human beings and the bodies of horses, fabrics, clothing and provisions. The felt carpet, with an area of 30 square metres (320 square feet), was originally on the wall of the log-built burial-chamber.

Henri Matisse
The Red Room. *1908*

→
Henri Matisse
The Dance. *1910*

57

Kees van Dongen
Red Dancer. *Ca 1907*

André Derain
Grove. *Ca 1912*

Chaïm Soutine
Self-Portrait with the Beard. *1916*

In *The Painter's Family* (1911) Matisse attempted a new interpretation of a traditional genre. Reflecting on the art of portraiture, he said that portraitists had been overtaken by photographers and therefore nothing remained for artists to do but to enhance colour and design in their depictions. When painting his own wife and children in the interior of a living room, Matisse first and foremost united in a single harmonious whole the ornament of the brightly coloured carpet, the design of the wallpaper and the geometric pattern of the chessboard using the large pure patches of colour — the red of the boys' shirts and the black of his daughter's dress.

The Dutchman Kees van Dongen (1877–1968) became a fashionable portrait-painter, revealing the extravagant, sinful life of Paris's artistic bohemians to the wider public. His heroines are *femmes fatales*, dangerous, aggressive, driven by determination to attract, conquer and seduce.

The landscapes of Maurice Vlaminck (1876–1958) are gaunt and dramatic. Although he went through the "trial by colour" of Fauvism, this artist nevertheless had a greater sense of an inner affinity

with Van Gogh and Cézanne. His palette is expressive and full of tension; his linear rhythms impulsive and staccato.

André Derain (1880–1954) shared a studio with Vlaminck in the Parisian suburb Chatou during the Fauve period. At first passionately devoted to the same ideas as Matisse, he soon took a rapid turn in the direction of Cubism. In his painting *The Grove* Derain's palette has become drab, twilit, composed of dull grey, brownish and greenish combinations in which the trees no longer look like bright flat patches.

The flowering of French art in the nineteenth and early twentieth centuries seems all the more outstanding when compared to the painting produced in neighbouring countries in the same period. The second-floor rooms overlooking the courtyard contain a relatively small display of art from German, Italy and other European states. Naturally it is difficult to compare collections that are tremendously different in quantity and quality, but despite their disparateness and randomness, these works by artists of other schools do make it possible to trace certain national peculiarities.

The collection of nineteenth- and early-twentieth-century German painting should be particularly singled out. The Hermitage possesses one of the world's finest sets of paintings by Caspar David Friedrich (1774–1840), one of the foremost representatives of German Romanticism. Almost all of the nine works came to Russia during Friedrich's own lifetime, offered by Friedrich first to Emperor Nicholas I and then to the poet Vasily Zhukovsky who was tutor to Nicholas's heir. *On a Sailing-Ship* (1818–19) is more poetic dream than reality. The man and the woman, who are shown seated on the prow of a ship with their backs to the viewer, are looking intently at the horizon that embodies the idea of the beautiful world created by their imagination.

The small, and to a large extent randomly formed, collection of Italian twentieth-century art is dominated by the work of modern sculptors — Greco, Manzù, Messina, Consagra — donated to the Hermitage by their creators.

Wassily Kandinsky
Winter Landscape. 1913

Among painted works are two still lifes by Giorgio Morandi, one of the most talented and inspired Italian masters.

On one landing of the Wooden Staircase, which links the collections of recent French, German and Italian art with the Oriental Department and the Department of Russian Culture, hang four works by one of the greatest artists of the twentieth century, Wassily Kandinsky (1866–1944). He was born and grew up in Russia, spent his best creative years in Germany, but died and is buried in France. His paintings are without nationality; they are a part of twentieth-century world art. These Kandinsky paintings, which include one of his acknowledged masterpieces, the monumental *Composition No 6* (1915), came into the Hermitage in 1948 after the closure of the State Museum of New Western Art in Moscow.

In the south-western part of the palace a set of living apartments has survived that were created for the marriage of the future Emperor Alexander II, then heir to the throne. The decoration of these rooms began at the same time as the work to restore the Winter Palace after the great fire and was finished by April 1841. The "new suite of the heir", as it was known, consisted of the apartments of his bride Maria Alexandrovna. The main state room of this suite was the White Hall created by Alexander Briullov. The architect found a superb solution for this huge hall with two tiers of windows decorated in shades of white. The moulded ornament included depictions of military trophies, mythological figures and scenes. Besides that, the hall was adorned by *bas-reliefs* of Jupiter and Juno, Apollo and Diana, Mercury and Ceres, Neptune and Vesta.

Caspar David Friedrich
On a Sailing-Ship
1818–19

The Winter Palace
The Golden Drawing-Room

The main imperial residence in Russia had an exceptionally broad range of functions. For a century and a half, the palace was the centre of political and ceremonial life, not only for St Petersburg, but for the empire as a whole: the focus of social and cultural events in the city. It was the setting for official rituals, festive religious services, balls, plays and concerts. The palace was home to the imperial family, their immediate retinue, and a huge staff. It was a tremendous household with an enormous number of kitchens, storerooms, ice-boxes, stoves and fireplaces — and, to keep it all going, an army of servants, cooks, stokers, tailors and seamstresses. The palace was subdivided into sets of rooms connected by location, common purpose or occupation by a particular person, and a certain style of architectural decoration. Each of these sets of apartments could be allocated to any function, but, although the occupier or decoration might change, their boundaries rarely did. When the palace was restored after the 1837 fire, living apartments were created for Emperor Nicholas I, Empress Alexandra Fiodorovna, the heir to the throne, other grand dukes and duchesses, and the Minister of the Imperial Court, as well as several "reserve sets of apartments" for exalted visitors and more distant relatives of the Tsar.

The adjoining Golden Drawing-Room was intended by Briullov as a contrast to the White Hall. The decoration of this room, according to the architect's concept, was supposed to form a sort of pair with the main drawing-room of Empress Alexandra Fiodorovna (wife of Nicholas I) — the Malachite Room, that was also called "golden" in the nineteenth century. In the Golden Drawing-Room of Maria Alexandrovna the walls and vault were originally covered in white artificial marble with only the delicate moulded ornament being gilded. The furniture was completely gilded; the panels painted in imitation of lapis lazuli, a deep blue semiprecious stone. The interior was completed by a marble fireplace decorated with a *bas-relief* and a mosaic picture framed by jasper columns. In the 1860s–70s the walls here were completely gilded over.

The Golden Drawing-Room now contains showcases for a unique collection of cameos and intaglios made by skilled Western European craftsmen from semiprecious stones with layers of different colours — cornelian, agate, chalcedony, amethyst and onyx. This is one of the largest collections in Europe.

The White Hall

Apollo Slaying Python
*Cameo. 16th century
Milan, Italy. By Alessandro
Masnago. Agate*

The Golden Drawing-Room

It was started by Catherine the Great who described her passion for such stones as a disease. In a brief span of time she bought the collections of the Duc d'Orléans, de Breteuil and Casanova which as well as highly valuable examples of European glyptic art also included works by ancient gem-cutters. Some of the cameos were produced in the workshop of the Browns, celebrated English craftsmen, to Catherine's personal commission.

As well as the state rooms, the private living quarters of Maria Alexandrovna — the Crimson Study, Boudoir, Blue Bedroom, Bathroom, Lavatory and Green Dining-Room — have retained their decoration.

One of the most exquisite is the Boudoir. Briullov's 1841 decoration of the room was completely replaced in 1853 by Harald Bosse in keeping with a new vogue for the Rococo style with delicate carved and gilded motifs, and virtuoso painted insets in the walls and ceiling. The architect used paintings from the Hermitage stocks as decoration above the doors. The Boudoir is given a special sense of intimacy by a sort of alcove, separated by a step, a low gilded railing and drapes. The architect originally wanted to stress this division by colour too, lining the walls of the alcove in white, and the rest of the Boudoir in crimson fabric. The deep red material used for the wall panels, upholstery and drapes for the windows and doors was commissioned from the Cortier factory in France.

Of particular interest in the west wing are the interiors that in the nineteenth century were regarded as memorial rooms. These rooms overlooking the Admiralty were decorated by Quarenghi in 1791 for Catherine's eldest grandson the future Alexander I. In 1793 the rooms were vacated as after his marriage Alexander and his bride lived in another part of the palace. Alexander's brother Konstantin lived in the apartments for three years, until his marriage, when they passed to the next brother, Nicholas. When he became Emperor, Nicholas I decided to continue the tradition and gave the rooms to his heir, the future Alexander II. Because of the special associations of these apartments in which three Russian monarchs grew up, their style of decoration was never changed. After the fire Briullov reproduced the interiors here "down to the last detail".

After the fire, rooms in the western wing of the Winter Palace that adjoins Maria Alexandrovna's apartments were allocated to the sons of Nicholas I — the heir to the throne Grand Duke Alexander (the future Alexander II) and his brothers, Konstantin, Nikolai and Mikhail.

The Emperor's own apartments were separated from those of the Grand Dukes by the long, narrow Dark Corridor — a service room in which guardsmen were on duty. Until the 1917 revolution its walls were hung with silver trays for offering bread and salt — the traditional Russian welcome ceremony — that were given to the Russian Emperors as mementoes of formal meetings with their subjects. From July 1917 the western part of the Winter Palace served as the residence of the Provisional Government. The Dark Corridor linked the reception rooms and offices of Prime Minister Alexander Kerensky with the clerks' offices. It was here that the historic storm of the Winter Palace took place. On the night of 24 October (7 November New Style) 1917 detachments of revolutionary soldiers and sailors entered the palace through "His Imperial Majesty's Entrance" (now the October Entrance) and made their way along the Dark Corridor to the Malachite Room which was being used for cabinet meetings. They arrested the Provisional Government and opened the way to the declaration of Soviet power.

Today the walls of the Dark Corridor are adorned with Western European tapestries of the seventeenth and eighteenth centuries. The Hermitage possesses an extremely rich collection of tapestries which are reminiscent of monumental painted panels in the complexity of their compositions and the wealth of different colours. The production of tapestries is an exceptionally difficult and painstaking business: in the course of a year an experienced craftsman could weave no more than one to one and a half square metres (11–16 square feet) of a picture.

*The Boudoir
Detail of the interior*

The Appearance of the Madonna. Tapestry from the Appearance of the Sablon Madonna series. From a cartoon by Bernard van Orley. 1518–19. Brussels, Flanders. Wool, silk

Proof of an Emperor Konstantin rouble (obverse). 1825 Russia. Silver

Proof of an Emperor Konstantin rouble (reverse)

At the present time in the western part of the Winter Palace can be found the displays of the Departments of Numismatics, the East and Russian Culture.

The Department of Russian Culture is the youngest in the Hermitage, having been established just before the Nazi invasion of the Soviet Union in 1941. The name derives from a special selection of exhibits that illustrate the history, culture and daily life of the Russian state from ancient times to the twentieth century. In the halls of the museum visitors can see a relatively small, but first-rate collection of Early Russian icons and fragments of frescoes, as well as the work of potters, weavers, the weapon-smiths of Tula and the ivory carvers of the North. And the Winter Palace itself, the architectural decoration of its rooms, the furniture, chandeliers, parquet floors and vases — all the remarkable complex created by the efforts of numerous architects, artists and craftsmen — is the priceless exhibit of this department.

The pride of the Hermitage collection are items from the time of Peter the Great. The core of them belong to the "Study of Peter the Great" that was kept in the Kunstkammer from the eighteenth century. In 1848–49 the exhibits in that study were transferred to the Winter Palace where a "Gallery of Peter the Great" was formed. We can judge about the great transformations brought about in Russia by Peter from the set of lathes designed by Andrei Nartov for the Tsar's own workshop, measuring instruments that Peter used, portraits of his companions-in-arms and contemporaries by Ivan Nikitin, Andrei Matveyev, Luigi Caravaque and Johann Tannauer, engravings of St Petersburg by Alexei Zubov. Among the finest works of sculpture produced in Russia are bronze busts of Peter and Prince Alexander Menshikov created by the Italian Bartolommeo Carlo Rastrelli (1675–1744) who was invited to Russia for three years by the Tsar but stayed the rest of his life. Rastrelli, father of the architect, also created the famous life-size wax figure of Peter the Great commissioned by his widow Catherine I immediately after his death in 1725.

A remarkable mosaic portrait of Peter, rightly considered one of the department's finest exhibits, was created in the 1750s by Mikhail Lomonosov. That

After the death of Alexander I on 27 November 1825, the throne should have passed to his eldest brother Grand Duke Konstantin. The Ministry of Finance began to prepare for the minting of new coins with the portrait of the new Emperor. Konstantin abdicated, however, in favour of the next brother, Nicholas, who became Emperor Nicholas I on 14 December 1825. The proof Emperor Konstantin coins were kept in the stores of the Ministry of Finance. In 1878 Alexander II distributed five silver roubles among collectors; one of them is now in the Numismatic Department of the Hermitage.

Bartolomeo Carlo Rastrelli
Emperor Peter the Great
1724. Russia

Grigory Musikiysky
Portrait of Catherine I
1827. Russia. Miniature

*Snuffbox. 1752. Russia
By Dmitry Vinogradov
Porcelain*

Vinogradov (*ca* 1720–1758) was a gifted research chemist, a friend of the great scientist Mikhail Lomonosov, and discovered the method of making porcelain. In the 1740s a factory was established in Russia where experiments were carried out to produce this precious form of ceramic, as the highly prized examples of Chinese, German and French porcelain were very expensive, while the secret of how to make them was carefully guarded. After long searching Vinogradov arrived at the composition of porcelain in 1747. The *Pugs Snuffbox* was produced at the Imperial Porcelain Works in St Petersburg using Russian raw material and the technology developed by Vinogradov.

great Russian scientist, writer and artist himself revived the technique of working in smaltos, small pieces of coloured glass.

The works of Russian art from the eighteenth and nineteenth centuries that abundantly decorate the living apartments in the western part of the Winter Palace form an effective whole in combination with the rich architecture of the interiors.

Particularly luxurious are the rooms created for Empress Alexandra Fiodorovna, the wife of Nicholas I. The Malachite Room was created by Alexander Briullov in place of Montferrand's Jasper Drawing-Room. Briullov retained the originally layout of the room with the placing of the columns and pilasters around the perimeter, but at the Tsar's request, other materials were used to finish the room. "Rich Siberia replaced its jasper with gold and malachite that were also its own," a contemporary wrote. As early as the eighteenth century malachite, then a great rarity, was used in craft work: to cover table ornaments, snuffboxes, writing sets and vases.

In the 1830s, following the discovery of huge deposits of the mineral at the Demidovs' copper mines in the Urals, malachite became more extensively used. In the Empress's state drawing-room the columns and fireplaces were worked in the difficult "Russian mosaic" technique: thin plates of stone were stuck onto the base, the joints between them filled with malachite powder and the surface then polished. The combination of these elements with gilding
had those who saw it in raptures, not knowing "what was more astonishing: the lavishness of the material or the lavishness of the artist's idea." The room

was furnished with pieces by Heinrich Gambs and enhanced by allegorical figures representing Day, Night and Poetry.

The Malachite Room was the boundary between the state rooms and the Empress's private apartments. It provided access to the Neva Enfilade that led from the State Staircase to the Throne Room. In the 1790s, with the construction of the new throne room (the St George Hall), this suite of rooms lost its original functions and was reconstructed to a plan by Quarenghi. In place of five old rooms he created three new ones: the Concert Hall, and the Large and Small Fore-Halls, the latter giving onto the Jordan Staircase, while in the decoration the unrestrained sumptuousness of the Baroque gave way to the refined austerity of Classicism. When he restored the Neva Enfilade after the 1837 fire Stasov retained Quarenghi's layout, but made the decoration of the rooms even more austere and monumental: the subtle play of superb combinations of colour in the artificial marble used to face the walls and columns was replaced by the solemn grandeur of white; minor decorative details disappeared and forms were enlarged.

The Concert Hall alongside the Malachite Room got its name from the fact that it was used for large concerts and theatrical performances. The room was decorated with depictions of the muses and Classical goddesses by the sculptor Josef Hermann and allegorical figures with attributes of the arts.

The Great Fore-Hall, the central element in the enfilade, is the largest state room in the palace. After 1856 it became known as the Nicholas Hall, as a large

Portrait of Empress Elizabeth Petrovna
By an unknown artist
Active in the late 1750s
Russia. Mosaic

The Malachite Room
Fireplace with malachite vases. Detail

The Malachite Room

The Small or White Dining-Room

Rooms in the north-western part of the palace were redecorated in 1894–95 for the new Emperor Nicholas II and his young bride Alexandra Fiodorovna (Princess Alix of Hesse-Darmstadt). The architect in charge of the work was Alexander Krasovsky (1848–1923). The decoration of the majority of the rooms occupied by the last Russian emperor was destroyed in the 1920s when the palace was converted for use as a museum. Only two, the dining-room and library, retained their appearance. In the White (Small) Dining-Room Krasovsky replaced Briullov's Pompeian style interior that had existed since 1839 with Rococo decoration featuring delicate moulded ornament in the form of seashells, garlands, scrolls, and the like. The furniture was produced from sketches by the architect Nikolai Nabokov. The superb stylization was complemented by authentic eighteenth-century items — tapestries produced at the St Petersburg factory (three allegorical parts of the world: *Asia*, *Africa* and *America*, and a decorative panel entitled *Swans*) and an English-made crystal chandelier. The Library of Nicholas II was stylized in the Gothic manner that was considered particularly appropriate for such purposes. The decoration of the Bremen sandstone fireplace features two heraldic beasts — the Romanov Gryphon and the Lion of Hesse, taken from the ancestral coats-of-arms of the Tsar and his spouse.

Silver tomb of Alexander Nevsky. 1750–53. The St Petersburg Mint

This distinctive monument to the thirteenth-century Prince Alexander Nevsky, an outstanding Russian military commander and statesman, who was later canonized by the Orthodox Church, was commissioned by Empress Elizabeth. Ninety *poods* (almost one and a half tonnes) of silver — a year's output from the Kolyvan mines in the Altai — went to create it. The tomb consists of a sarcophagus decorated with reliefs of scenes from Alexander Nevsky's life and his victories over foreign invaders. This is placed against a decorative pyramid that is crowned by the coat-of-arms of the sainted prince. Two angels, on the left and right sides of the pyramid, hold cartouches engraved with texts written by Lomonosov in praise of Alexander Nevsky and Empress Elizabeth. This unique ensemble is completed by two free-standing silver trophies and two censers.

*The Gothic Library
of Nicholas II*

equestrian portrait of the Emperor by the German artist Franz Krüger was installed there following his death.

For the richness of its decoration a contemporary aptly described the (Small) Fore-Hall as "an entrance hall, but an entrance hall worthy of the imperial house". (This was the first room off the landing of the Jordan Staircase.)

Another door from the great staircase led to a different "entrance hall" of a kind — the Field Marshals' Hall. This huge room was created by Auguste Montferrand in 1833–34 and restored by Stasov in 1838–39. It was used to display portraits of Russian field marshals: Rumiantsev, Potemkin, Suvorov, Kutuzov, Dibich and Paskevich. It acquired a certain inglorious fame from the fact that it was here, on 17 December 1837, that the fire broke out which ravaged the interior of the Winter Palace.

Even such a brief introduction to what is the great world of the Winter Palace has acquainted us with several pages in the history of the Russian imperial house and of the creation of a world-famous museum.

Leading from the Field Marshals' Hall, the Ministers' Corridor and a small passage connect the Winter Palace with the Hermitage buildings that appeared between the mid-eighteenth and mid-nineteenth centuries: the Small, Old and New Hermitages and the court Hermitage Theatre, completing a celebrated architectural masterpiece, the Hermitage palace complex.

The Field Marshal Hall

The Pavilion Hall
Detail of the interior

THE SMALL AND OLD HERMITAGES
THE HERMITAGE THEATRE

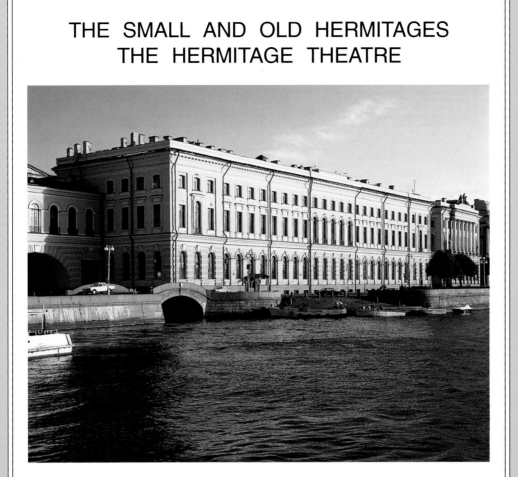

Looking along Palace Embankment, after the Baroque forms of the Winter Palace come the plainer Classical façades of several buildings with a shared historical name — the Hermitage. Constructed alongside the chief residence in the capital, the symbol of the highest authority in imperial Russia, the three Hermitages — Small, Old and New, together with the Hermitage Theatre, embodied another aspect of that authority: its intellectual and enlightened qualities.

The first foundation stone for the Hermitage was laid by Catherine the Great, who in the third year of her glorious reign resolved to have a Hanging Garden built by the Winter Palace and then, by that garden, two miniature pavilions and galleries to house her growing collections. Thus appeared the first product of Catherine's passion for building — the Small Hermitage. Conceived as a place where the Empress could withdraw into refined solitude from the fuss of ceremonial, it marked the beginning of a whole ensemble of edifices in which an empire of culture and art was born and flourished, an empire that Catherine passed on to her successors.

*Fiodor Rokotov. **Portrait of Catherine the Great.** Ca 1770*

The decoration of the Pavilion Hall was created to the plan by Andrei Stakenschneider in 1850–58. At the same time, in the adjacent part of the Hanging Garden, the architect created a winter garden. There, around an elegant fountain, tropical plants grew casting deep emerald shadows on the white marble arcades of the Pavilion Hall. Four "fountains of tears", in-spired by the original in the palace of the Crimean Khans at Bakhchisarai, raised poetic images of the Orient. Rich parquet and mosaic floors, a splendid set of chandeliers made of crystal and gilded bronze created an atmosphere of melancholy luxury in the garden. In 1939 the framework of the Winter Garden was dismantled, and now only the fountain, still occupying its former place, reminds us of it. At present the hall is used to display part of the Her-mitage's collection of mosaic tables from the mid-nineteenth century and the celebrated Peacock Clock by the noted eigh-teenth-century English clock-maker James Cox.

The Northern Pavilion of the Small Hermitage

The Hanging Garden of the Small Hermitage

The Pavilion Hall

Two talented architects —Jean-Baptiste Vallin de la Mothe (1729–1800) and Yury Velten (1730–1801) — created the Small Hermitage. The former designed it, the latter skilfully made the design a reality between 1764 and 1775. Still today a wonder of the world survives here: the Hanging Garden raised on lofty vaults, laid out with paths and flower beds and decorated with pieces of scul-pture. At the same time as this "upper garden" was being produced, on its southern edge Velten constructed a pavilion for the Empress's favourite, Count Grigory Orlov, and linked it by an aerial walkway to her personal apartments. This Little Palace, or Southern Pavilion as it was later called, retained its original appearance for much of its history.

Following the Southern Pavilion, a Northern, or Orangery, Pavilion appeared at the other end of the Hanging Garden in 1769. This pavilion at second-storey level con-tained the Orangery, a hall with two tiers of windows, five studies and the "Hermitage", a room with a table that could be raised and lowered where, undisturbed even by servants, Catherine and a select group of friends could enjoy "Small Hermitages", amusing evenings of reading, conversation, performances and games, in which the hostess and her guests participated as equals. Soon the name of these evenings became extended to the whole building. This name remained even when the pavilion was reconstructed in the middle of the nineteenth century. A special feature of the Small Hermitage are the galleries that run along three sides of the Hanging Garden. While the construction of the Orangery was still underway, Catherine herself came up with the happy idea of uniting the northern and southern pavilions with galleries that were then used to house the paintings the Empress had acquired from the Berlin merchant Johann Ernst Gotzkowsky. (This work was directed by Velten and succes-sfully completed by 1775.) With the years the works on display in these galleries changed, and they acquired names accordingly. In the middle of the nineteenth century the western gallery became known as the Romanov Gallery, because a portrait gallery of members of Russia's ruling house was installed there. The one flanking the Hanging Garden on the east acquired the name Peter Gallery or Gallery of Views of St Petersburg; the one on the east side either the French Gallery or the Gallery of Gems and the Cabinet of Peter the Great.

Today the Southern and Romanov Galleries of the Small Hermitage contain the collections of mediaeval Western European applied art and fifteenth- and sixteenth-century painting from the Low Countries. The stock of works by old Netherlandish masters is not great, but it gives an adequate picture of artistic culture in that centre of the North European Renaissance.

A diptych by Robert Campin (*ca* 1380–1444) — a *Madonna and Child* on the right panel, a *Trinity* on the left — numbers among the finest works by the artist.

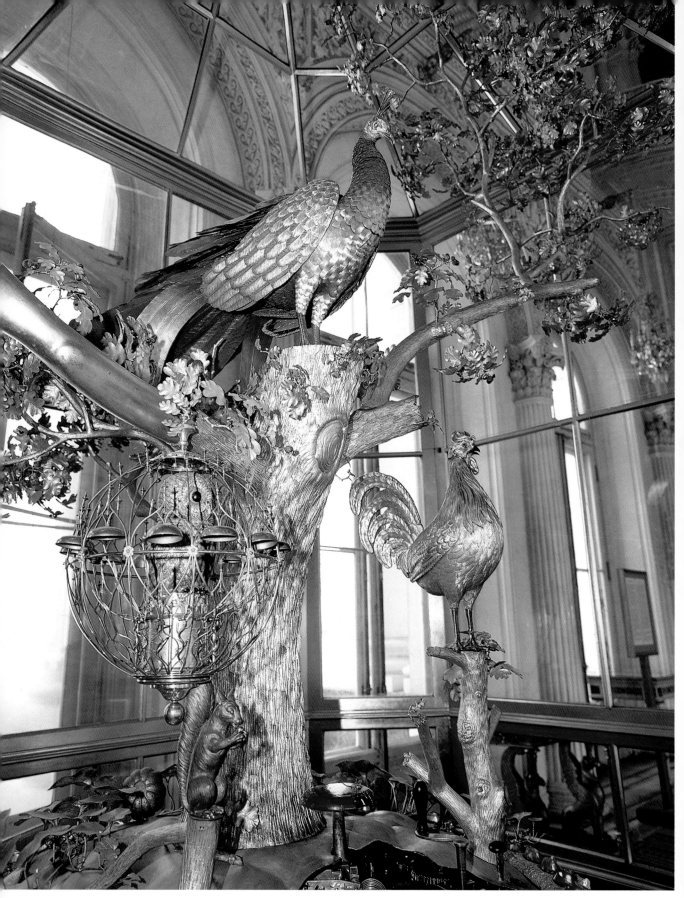

Clock: **Peacock.** *2nd half of the 18th century. England. By James Cox*

Clock: **Peacock.** *Details*

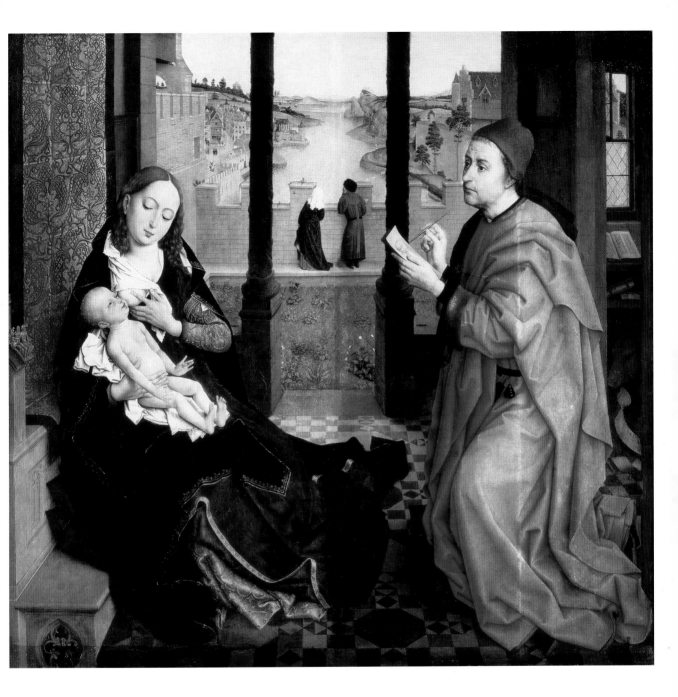

In his depiction of the Virgin Campin still followed the mediaeval tradition and did not idealize her image. The painting is full of everyday objects typical for life in the Low Countries, but every carefully and accurately painted detail here also has a hidden meaning of religious symbolism.

Rogier van der Weyden (*ca* 1400–1464), a pupil of Campin, is represented in the Hermitage collection by *St Luke Drawing the Virgin*. The artist attentively and reverently studies the beautiful, tender face of Mary, who is feeding the Christ-Child with her breast, and the calm, concentrated figure of the apostle. The landscape visible outside the room is an entire world crammed with vivid details that seem to have been painted from life.

From the display of paintings representing the Netherlandish school we return by the Romanov Gallery to the Pavilion Hall. From there we have a view through

Rogier van der Weyden
**St Luke Drawing
the Virgin**
Mid-15th century

Robert Campin
The Madonna and Child
1430s

*The Hall
of the Proto-Renaissance*

In Catherine the Great's time this was a billiard room. Later it was converted to house a display of Rembrandt's paintings and only acquired its present appearance in the mid-nineteenth century. At that time, following Stakenschneider's project, it was turned into the State Reception Room of the "seventh reserve set of apartments". The room owes its splendour to columns of green jasper, fireplaces, opulent pilasters with bronze decorations and painted inserts.
The doors are particularly impressive. They are made from precious varieties of wood and decorated with inset oval medallions of painted porcelain. Above the doors are painted panels *Times of the Day* by Michaly Zichy.

the passageway into the interior of the next building of the complex, the Old Hermitage. Constructed between 1770 and 1787, it was intended by the Empress as somewhere to house her growing collections of books and works of art. With this in mind, on the main floor of the building, on the side facing the Neva, Velten, the architect, placed an Oval Hall that was used to house Voltaire's library and beyond it a suite of rooms that accommodated the best works by Spanish, Italian and Dutch artists from Catherine's collection.

Simone Martini
**The Virgin from a scene
of the Annunciation**
*1330s. Right half of
a diptych*

The Nativity of Christ
*15th century. Florence
Workshop of Lucca della
Robbia. Majolica*

*Fra Angelico
Madonna and Child with
St Dominic and St Thomas
Aquinas. 1424–30*

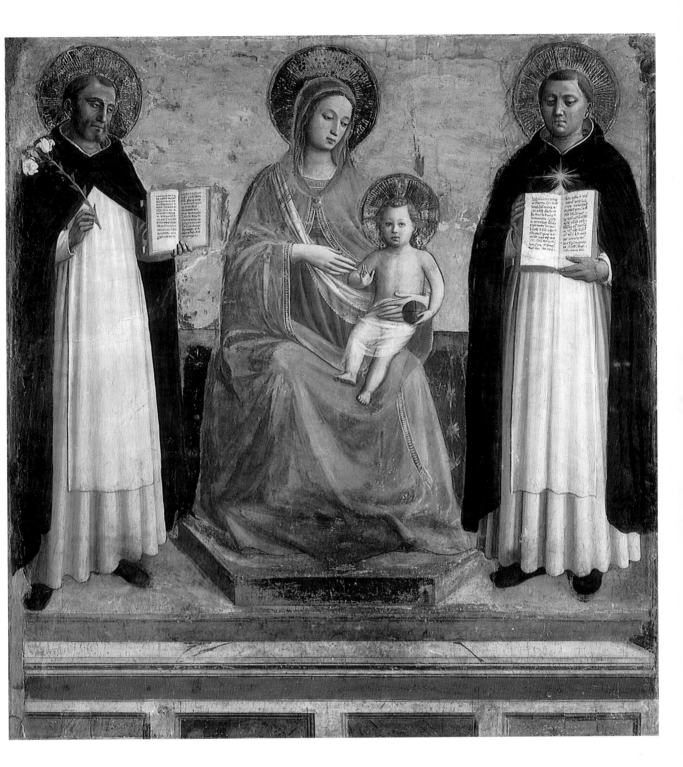

Three-quarters of a century later, when the New Hermitage was constructed just to the south and a large portion of the collections was transferred to that building, the function of these rooms changed. The architect Andrei Stakenschneider (1802–1865) converted them into apartments for the heir to the throne. The Oval Hall was replaced with a staircase, called the Council Staircase as the Council of State met on the ground floor here, while the rooms of the picture gallery turned into state drawing-rooms, bedchambers, reception rooms and studies.

This mid-nineteenth-century setting now houses one of the most celebrated parts of the Hermitage's collections — Italian art of the fourteenth to eighteenth centuries, including masterpieces of both Renaissance and Baroque eras. That tremendous period in human history, however, produced such an immense

Leonardo da Vinci
**The Madonna with
a Flower (The Benois
Madonna).** *1478*

*Boulle-technique doors in
the Leonardo da Vinci Hall*

wealth of art and artists that virtually no museum in the world can claim to pos-sess
works by all the great Italian masters of the time. The Hermitage is no exception.
Noteworthy among the works of the early or Proto-Renaissance is a masterpiece
created by the fourteenth-century Sienese master Simone Martini (1283–1344) —
the Virgin from a scene of the *Annunciation.* The painting is the right half of a diptych.
(The left half depicting the Archangel Gabriel is in the National Gallery, Washington.)

One of the greatest artists of the fifteenth century, Fra Beato Angelico da Fiesole
(*ca* 1400–1455) took monastic vows and for practically his entire career worked to
commissions from religious houses. In the 1420s he executed a series of frescoes
for a monastery at Fiesole near Florence. In the nineteenth century the monastery
was closed and the precious wall-paintings by Fra Angelico cut up into sections
and sold. *The Madonna and Child with St Dominic and St Thomas Aquinas*, the
central part of the composition, came into the Hermitage in 1882. This depiction
of the Madonna enthroned with saints at the sides derives from mediaeval tradition

Jacopo Palma
Portrait of a Man
Between 1512 and 1515

Giorgione. **Judith.** 1500s

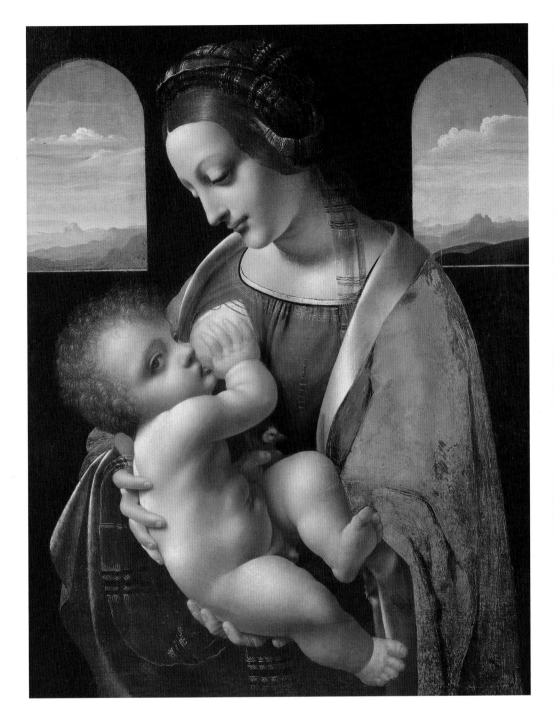

Leonardo da Vinci
**The Madonna and Child
(The Litta Madonna)**
Early 1480s

and is known as the *Sacra Conversazione* ("Holy Conversation"), but here the artist has given the saints a more earthly appearance.

The name of the fifteenth-century Florentine master Lucca della Robbia (1400–1482) is associated with the use of majolica — tin-glazed earthenware — to create sculptural reliefs, portraits, and multi-figure compositions that often adorned the walls of luxurious *palazzi*. We can get some idea of della Robbia's style from the relief of *The Nativity of Christ* produced in his workshop.

Dating from the High Renaissance, the period when Italian art reached its loftiest heights, are two paintings by Leonardo da Vinci, the same number by Raphael and Giorgione, nine works by Titian, and a sculpture by Michelangelo.

The *Benois Madonna* (*The Madonna with a Flower*) by Leonardo da Vinci (1452–1519) is among the earliest works by this artistic genius. The painting came into the Hermitage at the beginning of the twentieth century from the collection of the Russian architect Leonty Benois. It was executed in 1478 in oils, a technique that originated in the Netherlands and rarely used in Italy at the time. Leonardo has treated the traditional subject almost as a genre scene: the image of the Virgin is far from the ideal, there is nothing divine about it; this is rather a young Florentine woman playing with her child. The figures are given special weight, balance and elevated significance by the two sources of light from the side and the back.

The same qualities are also present in full measure in another masterpiece by Leonardo the *Litta Madonna* which came from the collection of the Milanese Duke of Litta. The stable composition, pithiness, almost mathematically attuned details and harmonious choice of colours do not obscure the subtle psychological reso-nance of the image — the gaze of a mother, full of tenderness, thoughtful and sad, as if with a premonition of her son's future sufferings. The painting would seem to have more traditional details than the *Benois Madonna* — the red and blue colour of the Virgin's clothing, the bird in the hand of the Christ-Child, symbolizing the spilt blood of the Saviour, but the ideal that the artist created became one of the greatest achievements of the High Renaissance.

Venice, the "Pearl of the Adriatic", made a significant contribution to the history of Italian painting. The very appearance of this splendid city, seeming to glitter with precious shades of colour, encouraged the emergence here of celebrated masters of colour. The High Renaissance opened in Venice with the name of Giorgione (Giorgio de Castelfranco; *ca* 1478–1510). Despite his brief life (the artist died at the age of 33 during a plague epidemic), Giorgione played a decisive role in the development of Venetian painting. *Judith* is among the generally acknowledged masterpieces of the Hermitage collection. Giorgione tackled the then popular theme of a heroic deed as the worthiest expression of human nature in the image of a beautiful young woman against a background of a bright landscape. Even the head of the Assyrian general Holofernes lying at Judith's feet and the sword in her hand do not disturb the sense of calm and purity that emanates from the figure of this heroine of the apocryphal story.

The peak of Venetian art in the Renaissance period is justly regarded as being the painting of Giorgione's pupil Titian (1485/90–1576). The best known works by the artist in the Hermitage were created towards the end of his long life. Titian tackled the story of *Danaë* on several occasion: the widespread use of Classical myths in this period was bound up with an aesthetic conception that originated

*Titian. **The Repentant Mary Magdalene.** 1560s*

The Hermitage Theatre

*The auditorium of
the Hermitage Theatre*

An additional attraction of the Hermitage Theatre is the memorial exhibition of the Winter Palace of Peter the Great. It was created in the lower storey very recently, in the second half of the 1980s, during the reconstruction of the theatre. Archaeological excavations uncovered architectural fragments of a palace erected in the late 1710s and 1720s. Quarenghi had preserved them in the foundation of his building and so provided the opportunity two hundred years later to recreate part of the courtyard, a gallery with a striking arcade and some of the interiors of the Winter Palace of the city's founder. And so two historical eras now co-exist in the Hermitage Theatre, permeated with the spirit of two great rulers, Peter and Catherine.

*The Room
of Chersonesus of Tauride*

in the Ancient World and held that the naked human body was the most beautiful creation of Nature. The proportions of the naked body of Titian's Danaë have something in common with the beauty of ancient statues, but they are infused with life by the mighty brush of the great sixteenth-century Venetian.

The Repentant Mary Magdalene is another of Titian's masterpieces. The beautiful sinner, presented in the act of unrestrained, impassioned repentance seems to have been woven from a wealth of glittering strokes of paint, glistening with deep shades of colour.

The extensive display of Italian fourteenth- to sixteenth-century art occupies all the main floor of the Old Hermitage building and ends at the meeting-point of the Theatre Staircase, the Raphael Loggias and the foyer of the Hermitage Theatre. At this point a striking "Venetian arch" thrown across the Winter Canal links the Hermitage buildings with one of the most exquisite components of the former imperial residence — the Hermitage Theatre. The decree ordering its construction was signed by Catherine the Great on 6 November 1783. Two years later, on 16 November 1785, an entry was made in the court journal reporting that the Empress and members of the imperial family "proceeded through the Hermitage to the new theatre where they watched the rehearsal of a comic opera…" The designer, and constructor within such a short period, of the new building was the noted Italian-born St Petersburg architect Giacomo Quarenghi. He has the honour of having created on the bank of the Neva a true masterpiece that became one of the finest palace theatres in Russia and indeed in Europe. The harmony and clarity of the Hermitage Theatre mark it out in the panorama of Palace Embankment, and it completes in a style "as exquisite as all the rest" the ensemble of Hermitage buildings. Behind the Classical façade of the building, which is particularly striking when viewed from the junction of the Neva and the Winter Canal, the architect installed a magnificent auditorium and stage. Taking his lead from Ancient Roman prototypes, Quarenghi designed the interior in the form of an amphitheatre and with his inherent sense of proportion decorated the proscenium arch and the walls with Corinthian semi-columns and niches, enriching the auditorium with sculpture in the form of heavenly and earthly gods of the theatre. The Hermitage Theatre played host to the finest Russian and foreign companies. It witnessed the brilliant talents of Ivan Dmitrevsky, Vera Samoilova, Fiodor Chaliapin, Mathilda Kschessinska and many other outstanding actors, singers and ballet dancers of the eighteenth to twentieth centuries. Still today the Hermitage Theatre retains for the most part its original appearance which splendidly combines the elegance and sense of intimacy proper to the private theatre of the imperial family.

THE NEW HERMITAGE

The New Hermitage holds a unique place in the architectural complex of museum buildings. It appeared at the behest of Nicholas I who recognized the necessity of constructing a special building capable of accommodating the art treasures belonging to the crown that were then scattered around the many palaces in the capital. The Tsar commissioned the plans for the "Imperial Museum" from the court architect of King Ludwig I of Bavaria, Leo von Klenze, who in collaboration with his Russian colleagues Vasily Stasov, Nikolai Yefimov and Alexander Briullov created a unique work of architecture.

Franz Krüger. **Portrait of Emperor Nicholas I.** *1827*

*Dish. 16th century
Deruta, Italy. Majolica*

The Hermitage has some 500 examples of Italian Renaissance majolica — magnificent and extremely expensive dishes, vessels and wine-coolers. They were made of earthenware covered with an opaque glaze, painted with bright colours and then fired again. These highly prized collector's items often feature reproductions of works by famous artists, including Raphael. In Italy there were several noted centres producing majolica, whose products differed in certain distinctive features. In Deruta, for example, majolica dishes were given a very thin lustrous over-glaze that gave the piece an iridescent metallic sheen. The formula for this overglaze was a carefully guarded secret.

Raphael
***The Conestabile
Madonna.*** *1502–03*

The Majolica Hall

The story of St Petersburg's Raphael Loggias is unique. In the late 1770s Catherine the Great commissioned copies of the famous frescoes executed by Raphael and his pupils in 1516–18 in the loggias of the Vatican Palace. The copies, made in egg tempera on canvas, were made by a team of artists led by Christoph Unterberger. A year later the architect Quarenghi arrived at the Russian court for the purpose of installing the copies in Catherine's winter residence. The careful measurements of the Vatican loggias that he made before leaving for Russia determined the choice of a site for the new extension. In 1783 work began on the construction of the gallery next to the (Old) Hermitage, alongside the Winter Canal. Eleven year later the works that have preserved the appearance of Raphael's unique creation were installed there. Half a century on, when the New Hermitage was built, the Raphael Loggias block was partially reconstructed so that its interior with the whole painted ensemble was incorporated into the museum building. And so, this great work of art that has been called "Raphael's Bible" enjoyed a second rebirth in the Hermitage.

The New Hermitage was an embodiment of the age's conception of the museum as a universal repository of the artistic experience of mankind. This idea determined the architectural structure of the New Hermitage, the first purpose-built museum in Russia. It even determined the decoration of the façades, for which von Klenze choose the Neo-Grecian style deriving ultimately from Ancient Greece. In keeping with the Emperor's wishes, all the halls of the museum, irrespective of the character of the items displayed, were decorated in a grand manner befitting the royal residence of which they formed a part. The lower storey of the building was allotted to the exhibition of ancient and modern sculpture, while the upper storey was mainly occupied by the collections of paintings belonging to the court. Everything was organized in a particular manner with the sole aim of compiling a universal, encyclopaedic picture of the history of world art. A museum within a museum, that is what the New Hermitage remains to this day, presenting a single cultural universe. Here different genres and art forms co-exist in surprising harmony. One of the most impressive is the Raphael Loggias ensemble, created in 1783–92 to satisfy the ambitious aspirations of Catherine the Great and incorporated into the Museum by Leo von Klenze half a century later. These superb copies of Raphael's frescoes (now all but lost) and their setting in the Vatican found a highly worthy place among the elaborate interiors of the New Hermitage.

Original works by the great Renaissance artist are displayed in the adjoining Majolica Hall. There, surrounded by colourful examples of Italian ceramic art from the sixteenth century, visitors can admire two painted masterpieces by Raphael (Raffaello Santi; 1483–1520).

Caravaggio
The Lute-Player. *Ca 1595*

Michelangelo
Crouching Boy. *1530s*
Marble

The Conestabile Madonna by Raphael was considered the gem of the collection held by Count Conestabile in Perugia. The decision to sell the work abroad raised such a storm of protest among the Italians that the Count, who was badly in need of money, was obliged to publish a special brochure explaining his reasons. The relatively small work is a *tondo*, a round painting. A young Virgin of exquisite beauty holding the Christ-Child with a book in her lap, is placed against the background of a panoramic landscape. The soft line of the hills, the mirror surface of the lake, the slender trees covered with light spring foliage — this poetic, entirely harmonious landscape is reminiscent of Umbria, the artist's native region. The picture is set in a sumptuous gilded frame that once formed a single whole with the image as it was carved from the same wooden panel (according to legend following a sketch by the artist himself) on which the work was painted. After this precious purchase arrived in the Hermitage in 1871, specialists discovered that cracks in the wooden base of the painting had grown and it was decided to carry out a difficult restoration operation — transferring the painting to canvas.

In 1504 Raphael moved from Perugia to Florence where the second Hermitage painting, *The Madonna with the Beardless Joseph*, was painted.

Practically all the finest works of Michelangelo (1475–1564), one of the greatest of the Renaissance titans, are in Italy. This brilliant painter, sculptor and architect is represented outside his homeland only by a few works. The *Crouching Boy* sculpture is the only work by Michelangelo in the Hermit-age. The light alternately flares up and dies on the rough piece of marble, as if stressing the tension that fills the compressed figure of the young man. Not the face, barely chiselled out, but the body with the muscles of the back and legs protruding powerfully, a compressed spring ready to straighten out, but pushed down seemingly by an unbearable weight, reveals the sculptor's concept.

At its basis lie the tragic reflections of the artist on a world that no longer has room for harmony and beauty.

It is believed that this sculpture was originally one of the decorative figures devised by Michelangelo to decorate the family mausoleum of the Medici rulers of Florence. One of the sketches for the decoration of the burial chapel does indeed contain depictions of crouching boys, placed at the top in niches above the tomb, that are reminiscent of the Hermitage statue. The artist seems to have later modified his concept, however, and the *Crouching Boy* was executed as a work in its own right. The statue looks unfinished, but scholars of Michelangelo's work are divided over whether the great sculptor did indeed abandon the piece, leaving the marble unpolished, or this was a consciously chosen method.

The Spanish Skylight Hall Torchère. 1805. Designed by Andrei Voronikhin Kolyvan Lapidary Works

The Small Italian Skylight Hall

The three large interconnected halls in the heart of the New Hermitage are known as the Skylight Halls. The name comes from the fact that they are lit from above through massive glazed areas in the ceiling. These tremendous rooms were specially designed by the architect to accommodate the monumental canvases produced by the Italian and Spanish schools between the late sixteenth and eighteenth centuries. A notable feature of the decorations in these rooms are items made of malachite, porphyry and lapis-lazuli. These vases, table-tops and torchères were produced at the Peterhof, Yekaterinburg and Kolyvan Lapidary Works.

The surface of the sculptor's later creations often look "churned up", something which gives them a special inner dynamism and drama.

The art of Michelangelo was the culmination of the Renaissance — the greatest stage in the history of art in the Modern Age.

Small rooms in the New Hermitage known as Cabinets, as well as the Large and Small Italian Skylight Halls contain works by Italian artists of the late sixteenth to eighteenth centuries. The peculiarities of the Late Renaissance in Venice are revealed in the monumental canvases by the followers of Titian: Paolo Veronese, Tintoretto, Jacopo Bassano, Jacopo Palma the Younger, hanging in the Small Skylight Hall. The Hermitage collection covers all the chief trends in Italian seventeenth-century art, including superb examples of work by the founders of the Bologna Academy, which became the prototype for such institutions around the world: the brothers Annibale and Lodovico Carracci, Guido Reni, Domenico, and Guercino. Among the Hermitage's masterpieces is its sole work by Caravaggio (Michelangelo Merisi da Caravaggio; 1571–1610). Caravaggio was the father of a powerful realistic tendency in seventeenth-century art, one of the forerunners of the Baroque. The influence of his painting on contemporaries can only be compared with that of the great Renaissance figures on their age. Caravaggio had devoted followers in other European countries: France, Spain, Holland and Flanders. *The Lute-Player* vividly reveals the innovative achievements of Caravaggio's art. By a deliberate heightening of the contrasts between light and shade, the artist attains an extreme sense of volume, an almost illusory materiality or sculptural quality in the painted form. The beautiful, soft face of the young musician, delicate, almost feminine hands and the soft lines of neck and shoulders stress the individuality of the model, while the fruit, sheet music, bouquet of flowers, violin and bow on the table have been painted with precision and verisimilitude. Yet this seemingly simple genre scene has a concealed allegorical message. Beauty and youth are soon lost: this is hinted at by the broken string on the bow and the crack in the table-top.

In the eighteenth century only the Venetian school continued to uphold the fame of Italian art. A pride of the Hermitage collection are works by the celebrated monumental artist and brilliant colourist Giovanni Battista Tiepolo, the landscape painters Antonio Canale and Francesco Guardi.

Eternally festive and beautiful as in a dream — that is how the lagoon city appears in *The Reception of the French Ambassador in Venice* by the virtuoso Antonio Canale (1697–1768), known as Canaletto. At the same time every element here is accurate, as is the historical event depicted. Venetian painters created a special type of architectural landscape marked by an almost photographic precision in the depiction of details, yet in their pictures the city remains full of the charm and mystery that still make it attractive today.

Two mighty and independent artistic centres — Holland and Flanders — emerged in Europe in the early seventeenth century. In the Hermitage they are represented by a collection of exceptionally quality and richness that contains paintings by almost all the leading artists of the century, that was the highest point in the history of these national schools.

Flemish painting s distinguished by a rare monolithic quality. In essence, its character and achievements were entirely determined by the work of the head of the school — Peter Paul Rubens (1577–1640). All Flemish artists were to one degree or another influenced by that great figure. Rubens' studio tackled anything and everything: painting from monumental decorative panels to landscapes and portraits, sculpture, architecture, applied art and was considered a real academy of art. Rubens established the life-affirming character of Flemish art that is founded on a rich colour scheme, temperamental dynamic movement and materially solid forms. *The Bean King* was created by Jacob Jordaens (1593–1678), a master of genre painting.

In the work of Frans Snyders (1579–1657) the still life lost its intimate quality

The Knights' Hall

The room now known as the Knights' Hall was created to display the imperial numismatic collection. The small-scale nature of the exhibits enabled von Klenze to introduce rich painted ornament in the decoration of the walls and ceiling, as well as panels of artificial marble. The painting was executed by Johann Drollinger and Daniel Jensen. After the collection of Western European arms and armour of the fifteenth to seventeenth centuries was moved here, the room acquired its present name.

Canaletto. **The Reception of the French Ambassador in Venice.** *1740s*

The Knights' Hall Display→

Jacob Jordaens
The Bean King. Ca 1638

The subject of this painting is the traditional festive meal at Epiphany, or the Feast of the Magi (6 January). An old Dutch tradition called for a pie with a bean baked into it to be served on that day and whoever found the bean in his portion became "the King of the Feast".

and became a monumental, dynamic celebration of the abundance of natural forms. *The Game Shop* is one of a series of four paintings commissioned for the Bishop of Bruges's dining-room.

A brilliant portrait painter sought by many including European monarchs, Anthony van Dyck (1599–1641) is represented in the Hermitage by more than twenty works. The artist's virtuoso *Self-Portrait* is full of refined artistry.

Rubens' own *Union of Earth and Water* (*ca* 1618) is a work painted with a dynamic, expansive freedom. It is an allegory in which the Earth goddess Cybele represents Flanders and her union with Neptune, the god of the sea, indicates the need to obtain access to the sea for the country to flourish.

The main customers for the works of Dutch painters in the seventeenth century were wealthy burghers who decorated their homes with depictions of daily existence, still lifes, portraits, and landscapes that were generally of no great size. It has therefore become customary to refer to their painters as "the small Dutch masters". These artists painted accurately and subtly, not prettifying but poeticizing the lives and daily round of their upright, sober-minded fellow citizens. Willem Claesz Heda (1594 – between 1680 and 1682) created a realm of astonishing beauty and harmony from everyday objects. In *A Glass of Lemonade* Gerard Ter Borch (1617–1681) turned a scene of procurement into a refined world glowing with precious shades of colour. *The Revellers* by Jan

The Snyders Hall

According to the original project, the Snyders Hall was to be used for a display of ancient medals and coins. Shortly before the opening of the New Hermitage, however, it was decided that large paintings by Russian artists would be hung in the room. At that point all the walls were lined with crimson cloth, completely covering the painted decoration. The display of Russian paintings remained in the room until 1897 when they were transferred to the new Russian Museum. Later seventeenth-century Flemish paintings were installed here, including the still lifes by Frans Snyders, whose name the room now bears.

Frans Snyders
The Game Shop. 1609

Anthony van Dyck. **Self-Portrait**
Late 1620s – early 1630s

Peter Paul Rubens. **The Union of Earth and Water.** Ca 1618

Peter Paul Rubens
Perseus and Andromeda. Early 1620s →

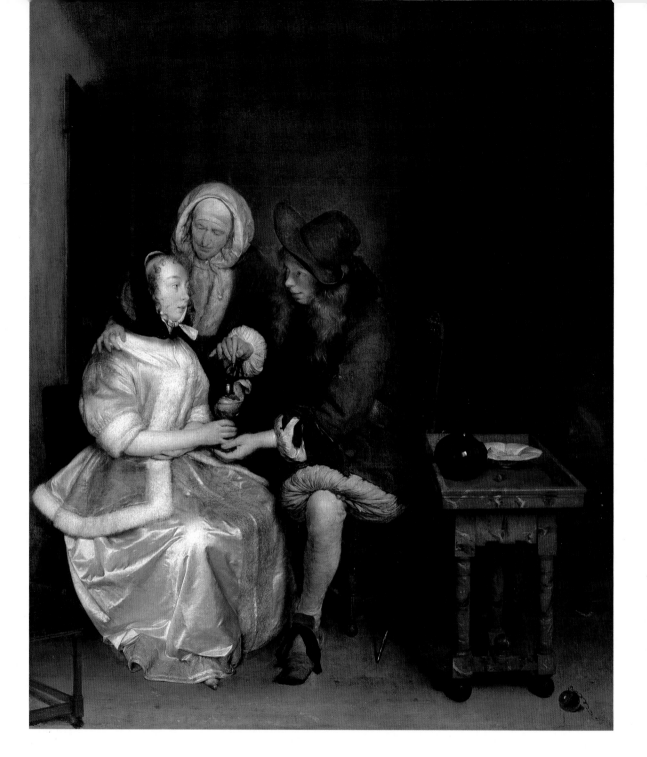

Steen (1626–1679) is full of humour and secretive, sly allusions. In *Portrait of a Young Man* the outstanding portrait-painter Frans Hals (1581/85–1666) seems to have captured a fleeting image in rapid motion.

The peak of Dutch painting comes in the work of one of the seventeenth century's greatest artists: Rembrandt van Rijn (1606–1669). The Hermitage possesses a priceless collection of over twenty paintings reflecting all stages of his dramatic career. *Flora* (1634) is a poetic depiction of Rembrandt's wife Saskia in the guise of the goddess of flowers and gardens. The artist is clearly feasting his eyes on his young spouse, dressing here in a luxurious festive dress and adorning her head with a wreath of flowers. In this happy time the artist was rich, loved and celebrated. Soon, however, Saskia died and that loss was followed by the gradual demise of wealth and fame. *Danaë*, a masterpiece completed after

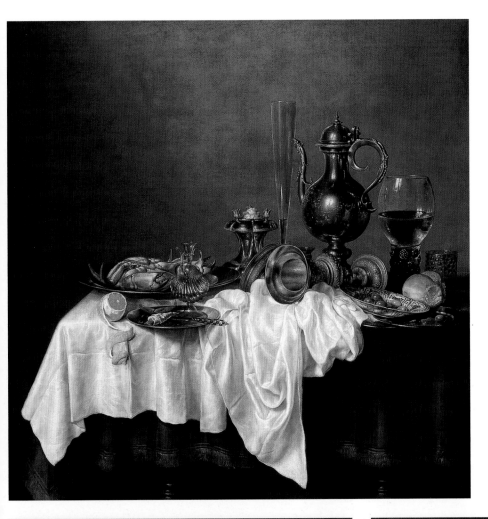

Gerard Ter Borch
A Glass of Lemonade
1660s

Willem Claesz Heda
Breakfast. *1648*

Frans Hals
**Portrait of a Young
Man with a Glove**
1660s

Jan Steen
Revellers. *Ca 1660*

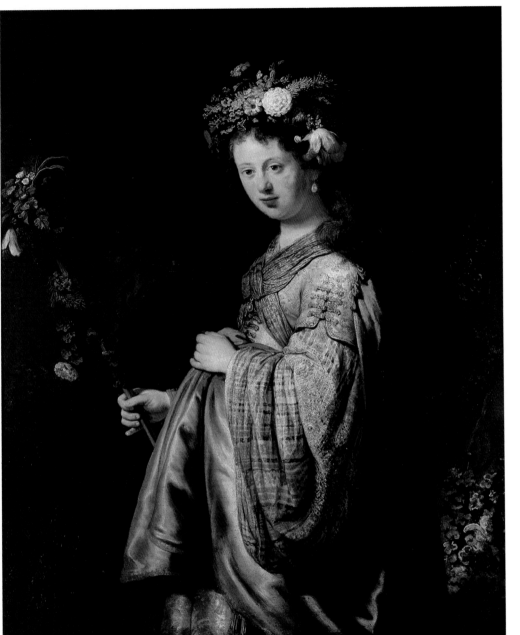

Rembrandt
Portrait of Saskia in the Guise of Flora. 1634

Saskia's death, lets us sense the cause of the conflict between the great artist and society. His works were too complex, too deep and psychological to be understood and properly appreciated by his contemporaries. *The Return of the Prodigal Son* draws the final balance of Rembrandt's life, as it were — the artist left alone, stripped of all earthly pleasures apart from the great capacity to create. The emotions that pervade all Rembrandt's work — love, suffering, forgiveness — here reach their greatest intensity.

The Golden Age of Spanish Art is customarily taken to be the seventeenth century, but it began as far back as the 1570s with Domenico Theotocopulos (1541–1614), a Greek-born artist who moved to Spain and became known as El Greco. The Hermitage canvas *The Apostles Peter and Paul* was the first of the *apostolados* series created in Toledo, works devoted to Christ and the twelve apostles. In a highly expressive manner — through colour, rhythm and movement — El Greco contrasts the highly dissimilar followers of Christ: Peter soft, wavering, full of doubt, and Paul certain that he is right and fanatically dedicated to Christian ideas. Among the greatest achievements of Spanish art in the seventeenth

Rembrandt
**Young Woman
Trying Earrings.** *1657*

Rembrandt. **Danaë.** *1636*

15 June 1985 was very nearly the last day in the existence of this masterpiece by the great Dutch artist.
The painting was splashed with sulphuric acid and slashed
twice with a knife. Specialist restorers urgently summoned
to the Rembrandt Hall found some places on the canvas
a bubbling brown mass. The painstaking restoration of
this priceless work lasted about ten years. The restorers
reinforced the surviving authentic layer of the painting and
carefully toned in the damaged areas with a layer of paint
close to Rembrandt's painted surface, entirely resisting the
temptation to reconstruct Rembrandt's manner of painting.
Now the work has returned to its public in the Hermitage.

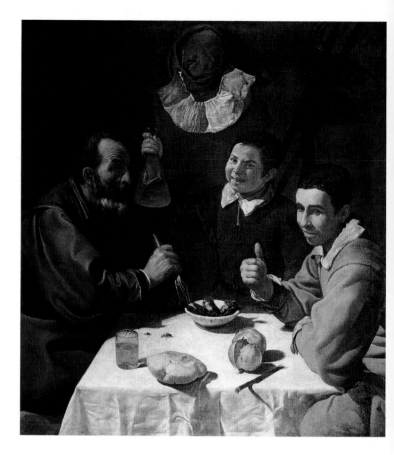

Francesco de Zurbarán
The Girlhood of the Virgin. *Ca 1660*

Diego Velázquez
Breakfast. *Ca 1617–18*

century are the works of Diego Velázquez, José de Ribera, Francisco de Zurbarán and Bartolomé Esteban Murillo. The oeuvre of Velázquez (1599–1660), the country's leading artist, court painter to King Philip IV, is represented in the Hermitage by two paintings. *Breakfast* by the eighteenth-year-old painter belongs to the *bodegón* genre that was exceptionally common in Spain and undoubtedly testifies to an enthusiasm for the work of Caravaggio. A *bodegón* (from the Spanish for "tavern") was usually an inn scene with typically Spanish figures sitting down to a modest meal, lit by a narrowly directed "Caravaggist" light that picks them out, as it were, from the semidarkness of the background. As with Caravaggio himself, this overtly humdrum subject in fact has several layers of meaning. The elements of the foreground still life —pomegranate, bread and glass of wine — are Christian symbols, while the boy, young man and old man were connected with the idea of the three periods in human life.

The artistic career of Francisco de Zurbarán (1598–1664) unfolded in the Andalusian capital Seville, a major cultural centre for the country. His paintings on religious subjects adorned the walls of many Sevillian churches and religious houses. Only a small number of works by this distinctive Spanish artist can be found outside his homeland. The Hermitage collection includes four of them. *The Girlhood of the Virgin* is one of the few intimate lyrical works from the brush of this usually austere and outwardly emotionally restrained master. Mary — a black-haired, dark-eyed Spanish girl — lit by a powerful stream of light pouring from above seems frozen in profound prayerful ecstasy.

The works of the last master of the Golden Age, Bartolomé Esteban Murillo (1617–1682) were the most popular products of Spanish painting with collectors and for that reason the Hermitage now has a significant number — seventeen, representing various periods in the artist's development. *Boy with a Dog* dates from his early period which was dominated by vivid images of little tramps, gypsies and beggars dressed in motley rags, but never loosing the immediacy in the expression of feelings that is typical of their age.

The great artist Francisco Goya (1746–1828), whose work around the turn of the nineteenth century marked the final end of the heyday of Spanish painting, produced the *Portrait of the Actress Antonia Sarate* donated to the Hermitage by the American collector Armand Hammer in 1974. Contemporary

El Greco. **The Apostles Peter and Paul.** *Between 1587 and 1592*

Pendant in the shape of swan. Spain. 16th century

*Pendant: **Caravel**
Spain. 17th century*

*Francisco Goya
Portrait of Antonia Sarate
Ca 1811*

*Bartolomé Murillo
Boy with a Dog. 1650s*

accounts suggest that Doña Antonia was more noted for her beauty than her talent. She died of consumption at the age of thirty-six and would probably have been forgotten, were it not for two attractive, animated portraits by Goya. The Hermitage portrait of the actress is an intimate depiction. The emotional, moving image of a young woman — a "portrait of the heart" as one art scholar put it — forms a kind of bridge between two eras, the parting age of great spiritual discoveries made by Velázquez and Rembrandt and the coming romantic age of Delacroix, Manet, Cézanne and Picasso.

The Gallery of the History of Ancient Painting is adorned by works from two of the most famous sculptors of the late eighteenth and early nineteenth centuries — the Italian Antonio Canova and the Dane Bertel Thorvaldsen who worked in Rome. In keeping with the enthusiasm for ancient art that arose in Europe in the

The Gallery of the History of Ancient Painting

Lying between the Grand Staircase and the Skylight Halls, this room serves as a foretaste of the Hermitage's painted treasures. Set into the walls are 86 paintings telling legendary stories of the birth of the arts in the Ancient World. Each was painted by Georg Hiltensperger using pigments mixed with hot wax on copper plates. A special effect is created by the domical vaults, some of which are crowned with lanterns providing diffuse lighting from above.

Antonio Canova
The Three Graces
1813–16. Marble

The Grand (Terebenin) Staircase

The upper landing of the Main Staircase. Decorative Western European sculpture of the first half of the 19th century

1760s, the Neo-Classical statues of Canova and Thorvaldsen display a perfect harmony of proportions and beauty of line while the surface of the stone has been very finely worked. The collection of works by Canova (1757–1822), the last great heir of Classical traditions in Italian art, numbers sixteen pieces. Canova was the most popular sculptor in Europe at the start of the nineteenth century. The best of the items in the Hermitage came from the celebrated collection of Empress Josephine kept at the Malmaison Palace outside Paris.

The celebrated marble *Three Graces* was created to Josephine's commission in 1816, but the former Empress died without ever seeing it. The group, which contemporaries regarded as the finest embodiment of the new ideal of beauty, passed to Josephine's son, Prince Eugène de Beauharnais, who subsequently married one of Nicholas I's daughters.

The ground-floor halls of the New Hermitage contain the collection of ancient art. This collection is divided into two parts. The first consists of works from Ancient Greece and Rome that came with various eighteenth- and nineteenth-century acquisitions; the second contains items found during excavations of Greek colonies on the northern Black Sea coast. Although rich and varied, the Hermitage collection is not evenly composed. The most precious items are the collections of Roman sculptural portraits and decorative sculpture; ancient cameos and intaglios; gold jewellery from burials in the Black Sea area; and the collection of painted vases. The valuable examples of sculpture and vases come in the main from the collection of the Italian Marchese Campana acquired at auction in Rome in 1861. As a result of immoderate spending on the purchase of ever more pieces, the Marchese, one of the greatest collectors of antiquities, ruined himself and, unable to settle his debts, was sentenced to twenty years hard labour. He had already offered his collection to Nicholas I in the 1850s, but with the chief proviso that the Tsar

Vessel in the form of
a sphinx. 5th century B.C.
Phanagoria, Black Sea
coast. Painted earthenware

**Hercules Fighting
the Lion.** Roman work
based on an original
created by Lysippus in
the 330s B.C. Marble

take it as a whole. The Hermitage did not agree to such conditions at that time; Nicholas wanted only a part of the antiquities. Before the auction the Hermitage was accorded special rights to chose some of the works in advance, as a result the Campana collection was divided between Russia and France. Gedeonov, the director of the Hermitage bought about six hundred items — more than a hundred sculptures and 500 painted vases — paying 6,000 Italian *scudi*. That is the story behind the creation of the Department of the Ancient World in the Hermitage.

The Dionysus Hall was specially created to house the imperial collection of ancient sculpture. Von Klenze stylized it in imitation of an ancient gallery: the side walls are faced with red artificial marble and divided up by massive columns; the floor is covered with a multicoloured mosaic, while the coffered ceiling is also authentic in type. The ancient marble sculptures are particularly effective when seen in such an architectural setting. The hall acquired its present name from a statue of the Ancient Greek god of wine and fertility dating from the fourth century B.C. included in the display here.

The sculpture of Ancient Greece, like its architecture, has for all the centuries since been considered the highest measure of beauty in art. In the Hermitage it is mainly present in the form of Roman copies. The finest example of the ancient ideal of beauty to be seen in the museum is reckoned to be the Tauride Venus, based on an original of the third century B.C. — the late, Hellenistic period of Ancient Greek art. The figure of Venus with deliberately elongated propor-

The Tauride Venus
Roman copy from a Greek original. 3rd century B.C. Marble

The Aura Hall →

tions, a small, exquisite head on a long willowy neck completely accords with the ancient ideal in which the spiritual and physical aspects are in harmonious union.

Ancient Greek statues were brightly painted, but that has been lost in the course of time. We can obtain some idea of how they must have looked to delighted contemporaries from the much smaller elaborately shaped earthenware vessels from the fifth century B.C. found in a burial mound at the site of Phanagoria, an ancient city on the Taman peninsula (to the east of the Crimea). One vessel in the form of a sphinx is a fascinating combination of a beautiful female face with pink skin, blue eyes and golden curls, the body of a lion and the wings of a bird.

The collection of Greek and Roman vases contains some 15,000 items, an undoubted masterpiece among which is the *Swallow Pelike*, a red-figure vase attributed to a craftsman named Euphronios. It depicts a man, a youth and a boy welcoming the appearance of the swallow as a sign that winter is over. An inscription on the base reports their conversation. "Look, a swallow!" the man exclaims. "Yes, by Heracles," the youth answers. "Here it is, spring," the boy declares.

The room known as the Jupiter Hall houses the Hermitage's best examples of Ancient Roman sculpture. The monumental statue of the great god here is of astonishing size. It dates from the first century B.C. and was discovered during excavations of a temple near Rome. Soon it was offered to Catherine the Great, through middle-men, but she suspected fraud and declined. Nevertheless the statue was destined to find its way to the Hermitage, arriving as part of the Campana collection.

Portrait of a Roman
*1st century B.C. Rome
Bronze*

The creator of this bust
has become known as
"the sculptor of the
Leningrad bronze", proof
of the high quality of this
work from the period when
the tradition of the Roman
sculptural portrait was
only forming.

The Kolyvan Vase Hall

Originally this hall was intended for a display of modern sculpture. In 1850, however, while the New Hermitage was still being built, a unique green jasper vase was installed here. It was made at the Kolyvan Lapidary Works to the design of the architect Avram Melnikov. Siberian stone-cutters worked fourteen years to produce the vase from a single block weighing nineteenth tonnes. It was delivered to St Petersburg on carts drawn by about 160 horses.

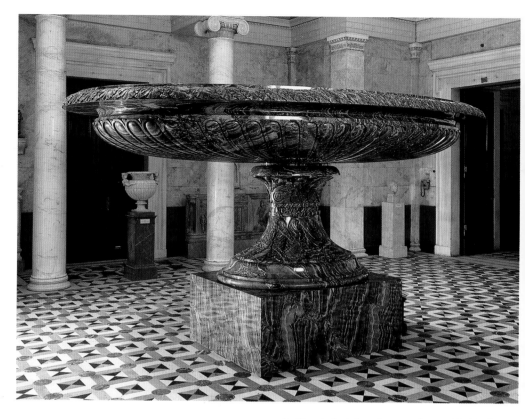

The Jupiter Hall

Jupiter. *Late 1st century B.C. Rome. Marble, bronze*

Statues like this one were created for many temples of Jupiter, the highest deity in the Roman pantheon. Ancient accounts suggest that the first depiction of Zeus (the Greek equivalent) in the form of a powerful, well-built, handsome man seated on a throne with a small figure of Nike, the goddess of victory, in one hand and a sceptre in the other was produced by the great Greek sculptor Phidias for the temple at Olympus. That wooden statue of Zeus decorated with gold and ivory was one of the wonders of the Ancient World. Sadly, we can judge it today only from later marble copies.

The heyday of Ancient Roman sculpture came in the second and third centuries A.D. and is associated with the sculpted portrait. The Hermitage collection, with some 120 such likenesses, is considered one of the best in the world.

The decorative formality of the official commissioned portrait does not obscure the subtle psychological characterization in the image of Lucius Verus, who was co-ruler with Emperor Marcus Aurelius. The stamp of uncertainty and anxiety lies on the plain, puffy face of Emperor Balbinus, who ruled briefly in 238, and a coarse, masterful look to the portrait of the soldier-emperor Philip the Arabian who came to power in the middle of the third century. The last two date from the troubled period of decline that foreshadowed the collapse of the Roman Empire.

A passageway created only in the twentieth century links the halls of the New Hermitage with the Winter Palace. It has become a sort of bridge connecting the Greek and Roman exhibits to the Ancient Egyptian collection. The Hermitage's stock of artefacts from that very early centre of human civilization

The Arrival of the First Swallow. Red-figure pelike 6th century B.C. Greece. By Euphronios Earthenware

The Twenty Column Hall

The interior here reproduces the inside of an ancient temple. The space is divided into three aisles by two rows of Ionic columns made from Serdobol granite. The original name of the room — the Hall of Greek and Etruscan Vases — indicates the display which the decoration was intended to suit. The walls feature motifs stylized in imitation of the painting on ancient lacquered vases. They were created by the painters Fiodor Wunderlich and Piotr Shamshin. The unique mosaic floor was produced at the Peterhof Lapidary Works.

is comparatively small, but the works in it — examples of monumental stone sculpture, small-scale plastic art, fragments of wall reliefs and papyruses, wood and stone sarcophagi, and mummies — give the visitor an idea of all the stages in the development of Ancient Egypt from its origins to its demise.

The State Hermitage owns several thousand works by European and Asian gold- and silversmiths. Today two specially equipped departments — the Treasure Gallery-1 and the Treasure Gallery-2 – have been opened for the public. The first of them is based on the Treasure Gallery of the Imperial Hermitage,

Amphora. 4th century B.C.
Chertomlyk burial mound
Silver

This splendid example of
a Greek-made wine vessel
was found in a Scythian
grave close to the town
of Nikopol in the Ukraine.
All the gold relief-work
that adorns it strongly
expresses the world
of Scythian symbolism.

Plaque in the form of panther from the Siberian collection of Peter the Great. Scythian. Gold 7th–6th century B.C.

Comb. 4th century B.C. Solokha burial mound Gold

but also includes the articles created in the new times. The second section displays the artifacts that entered the museum as a result of archaeological excavations.

The Treasure Gallery-1 begins with mediaeval objects – crosses, monstrances, staff finials, caskets, tabernacles and chalices. They are related to the church everyday life — as for instance, the silver-gilt reliquary shaped like the figure of a deacon and adorned with gems, an outstanding example of the culture of the Romanesque period (France, late 12th century).

Russian church art is represented by richly decorated Gospels and icons in golden mounts as well as a number of other precious articles. Worthy of special note among them are two liturgical sets commissioned by Tsar Fiodor Alexeyevich, the elder brother of Peter the Great, for the Cathedrals of the Saviour and the Resurrection in the Moscow Kremlin in 1677–79.

The imperial collection included secular pieces of jewellery, the earliest of which were various pendants created in the Western Europe in the seventeenth century. One of them, featuring the globe with a ship belonged to the famous pirate Francis Drake.

In the seventeenth century a fashion for tobacco sniffing became widespread. The collection of the museum has many snuffboxes, including two pieces that belonged to Peter the Great. This snuffbox,

Deer. *7th–6th century B.c. Burial mound by the Cossack settlement of Kostromskaya. Gold*

executed in the shape of a Dutch schooner, with the decoration of gold and mother-of-pearls, accompanied the Tsar in his travel abroad.

Empresses Anna Ioannovna and Elizabeth Petrovna did not spare money for the acquisition of luxury objects. The golden toilet set from Augsburg (1730) strikes us by its number of items – it contains 46 pieces. No less remarkable are the wonderful "bouquets" created by the French jeweller Jérémie Pauzié. Their central flowers are usually either a large amethyst faceted like a tulip or wonderful chrysolites or sapphires framed with diamonds. The same period saw the acquisition of large number of golden pocket watches and chatelaines of English work.

The reign of Catherine the Great has also left us fine collections of cameos, snuffboxes, bonbonières and patch boxes. The Empress used to purchase a large number of them from the best jewellers abroad. She also bought for her "*hermitage*" many precious objects, the collecting of which became then fashionable at the court.

One of the completing sections of the display of jewellery is a collection of pieces created in the late nineteenth and early twentieth centuries by the celebrated Carl Fabergé and by jewellers of his company. Truly unique is a miniature copy of the imperial regalia created for the World Exhibition of 1900 in Paris.

The display of the Treasure Gallery-2 begins with the Siberian Collection of Peter the Great – Russia's earliest collection of golden artefacts. They have mainly come from the burials of nomadic tribes related to the Scythians who inhabited the south of Siberia in the seventh century B. C.

The next rooms are devoted to masterpieces of Scythian goldwork (late 1st millennium B.C.) discovered in the ancient burial mounds of Kuban, Stavropol, the Urals, and East Siberia as well as the golden jewellery found in the necropolises of the ancient colonies on the Northern Coast of the Black Sea.

Small metal plaques from the Siberian Collection of Peter the Great. 4th–1st centuries B.C. Gold, turquoise

The Siberian Collection of Peter the Great was established on that Tsar's orders in 1715 and consisted of gold artefacts found in burial mounds in Siberia and the Altai mountains. The collection was displayed in the Kunstkammer (the museum Emperor Peter the Great founded). The identity of the tribes who created these burial mounds is unknown, but the pieces of jewellery found there bear a strong resemblance to the Scythian Animal Style.

Temple pendant bearing the head of Athene 4th century B.C. Kul-Oba burial mound. Gold

In 1830 soldiers cutting stone on the slope of a mountain near Kerch came across an extremely rich tomb of Greek origin in which a noble Bosporan, his wife and a slave armour-bearer were buried. Among the many first-rate items of jewellery found at this site were these superb elements of a woman's head-dress.

*Box for beauty spots
bearing the monogram
of Empress Elizabeth
Late 1740s.
By Jérémie Pausier (?).
Gold, diamonds*

Such small, flat containers
with a mirror inside the lid
were an essential fashion
accessory for a society lady
of the mid-18th century.
They were used to keep
artificial moles of black
taffeta, velvet or paper
which women applied
to their faces, necks or
breasts when attending
balls and public functions.
A beauty spot could be
used to disguise some
imperfection on the skin,
but more often it had
another purpose. At that
time there was even
a special, highly explicit
language of beauty spots,
that was, however, known
only to the initiated.
A spot in the middle of
the forehead, for example,
suggested "majesty"; one
at the corner of the eye
"passion"; one near
a dimple on the cheek
"jollity"; one on the lip
"coquetry". At a ball
particularly practised ladies
would use the mirror to
swiftly change the position
of their beauty spots, thus
revealing their secret
desires to their chosen
partner.

*Bouquet of gems in a glass
vessel. Late 1750s
By Louis David Duval
Amethyst, diamonds,
emeralds, rubies, Dutch
topazes, pyropes, spinel,
aquamarines, turqouise*

The last section of the Treasure Gallery-2 is devoted to the jewellery of China, Turkey, Byzantium and Central Asia. A place apart is given there to valuable diplomatic gifts presented to the Russian Emperors.

Thus peacefully co-existing within a single museum space, numerous Hermitage exhibits serve as vivid illustrations to the complex and interesting history of world culture.

Foreword by Mikhail Piotrovsky
Introduction by Vladimir Matveyev
Selection and text by Sergei Vesnin,
Sophia Kudriavtseva and Tatiana Pashkova
English translation by Paul Williams
Designed by Nikolai Kutovoy
Colour correction by Liubov Kornilova
Computer type-setting by Yelena Morozova
Photographs by Darya Bobrova, Leonid Bogdanov, Pavel Demidov,
Sergei Falin, Alexander Gronsky, Leonard Kheifets, Victor Savik,
Georgy Shablovsky, Vladimir Terebenin and Oleg Trubsky
Edited by Maria Lyzhenkova and Valery Fateyev (English translation)
Managing Editor Sergei Vesnin

THE STATE HERMITAGE
PLANS OF THE EXPOSITIONS

WINTER PALACE

SMALL HERMITAGE

OLD HERMITAGE

NEW HERMITAGE

Palace Square

General Staff

Winter Palace

New Hermitage

Small Hermitage

Old Hermitage

Neva River

GROUND FLOOR

Admiralty

Palace Square

Milliomaya Street

Neva River

Winter Canal

Main Entrance

Ticket desk

FIRST FLOOR

Admiralty

Palace Square

Millionnaya Street

Winter Canal

Neva River

State Rooms and Living Apartments of the Winter Palace
Rooms of French Art: 15th to 18th Century
Rooms of German Art: 15th to 18th Century
Rooms of English Art: 16th to 18th Century
Rooms of Russian Culture and Art

Rooms of Netherlandish Art: 15th and 16th Centuries
Rooms of Italian Art: 14th to 18th Century
Rooms of Spanish Art: 15th to 19th Century
Rooms of Flemish Art: 17th Century
Rooms of Dutch Art: 17th Century

189 — Malachite Room
191 — Nicholas Hall
193 — Field Marshals' Hall
194 — Peter the Great Hall (Small Throne Room)
195 — Armorial Hall

197 — Gallery of 1812
198 — St George Hall
204 — Pavilion Hall
214 — Leonardo da Vinci Room
227 — Raphael Loggias

230 — Michelangelo Room
238 — Large Italian Skylight Hall
243 — Knight's Hall
246 — Van Dyck Room
247 — Rubens Room

254 — Rembrandt Room
259 — Hall of Western European Mediaeval
       Decorative and Applied Art
271 — Great Church

SECOND FLOOR

Rooms of French Art: 19th and 20th Centuries

Rooms of German and Other European Art:
19th and Early 20th Centuries

Rooms of Italian Art: 20th Century

Rooms of the Culture and Art of the East
(China, India, Indonesia, Iran, Syria, Byzantium)

Numismatics Department

1   The State (Jordan) Staircase
2   The State (Terebenev) Staircase
3   Council Staircase

Cafe
Cloakroom

English edition

Palace Square

Admiralty

Neva River

Exit

Entrance

333
348
347
346
345
344
343
342
336
316
315
320

315 — Rodin Room
316–320 — Rooms of the Impressionists
     and Post-Impressionists
333 — Kandinsky Room

336 — Morandi Room
342 — Friedrich Room
343–346 — Matisse Rooms
347–348 — Picasso Rooms